10 minutes a day!

Word Ladders for Fluency

Photocopiable activities to boost reading, vocabulary, spelling and phonics skills

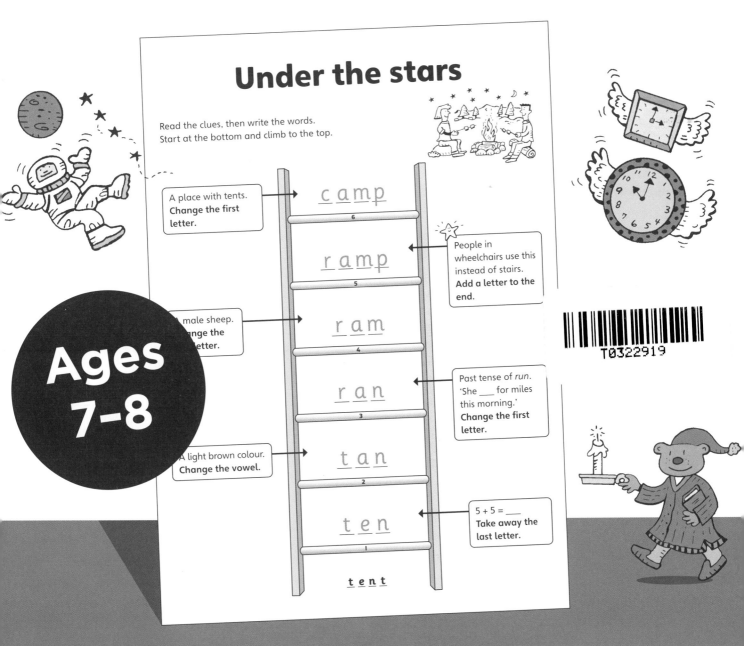

Under the stars

Read the clues, then write the words.
Start at the bottom and climb to the top.

A place with tents. **Change the first letter.**

c a m p
6

r a m p
5

People in wheelchairs use this instead of stairs. **Add a letter to the end.**

A male sheep. **Change the first letter.**

r a m
4

r a n
3

Past tense of *run*. 'She ___ for miles this morning.' **Change the first letter.**

A light brown colour. **Change the vowel.**

t a n
2

t e n
1

5 + 5 = ___ **Take away the last letter.**

t e n t

Ages 7-8

T0322919

Written by Timothy V. Rasinski

Edited by **Herts for Learning**

Published in the UK by Scholastic Education, 2022

Scholastic Distribution Centre, Bosworth Avenue, Tournament Fields, Warwick, CV34

Scholastic Ireland, 89E Lagan Road, Dublin Industrial Estate, Glasnevin, Dublin, D11 HP5F

SCHOLASTIC and associated logos are trademarks and/or registered trademarks of Scholastic Inc.

First published in the US by Scholastic Inc, 2005
Text and illustrations © 2008, Timothy V. Rasinski
© 2022, Scholastic

A CIP catalogue record for this book is available from the British Library.

ISBN 978-0-7023-0935-9

Printed by Bell & Bain Ltd, Glasgow
This product is made of FSC®-certified and other controlled material.

Paper made from wood grown in sustainable forests and other controlled sources.

1 2 3 4 5 6 7 8 9   2 3 4 5 6 7 8 9 0 1

Author
Timothy V. Rasinski

Editorial team
Rachel Morgan, Vicki Yates, Tracey Cowell, Julia Roberts

Design team
Ellen Matlach for Boultinghouse & Boultinghouse, Inc.
Justin Hoffmann, Couper Street Type Co.

Illustration
Teresa Anderko

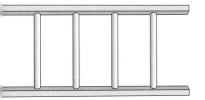
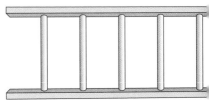

Contents

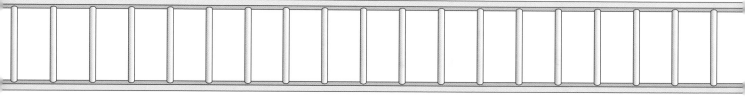

Foreword

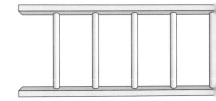

In the UK, the first stage of teaching reading focuses on phonics, with an emphasis on children learning to decode the words on the page. The essential skills of language knowledge, fluency and comprehension are developed alongside.

The National Curriculum states: 'Good comprehension draws from linguistic knowledge (in particular of vocabulary and grammar) and on knowledge of the world.' and that 'Skilled word reading involves both the speedy working out of the pronunciation of unfamiliar printed words (decoding) and the speedy recognition of familiar printed words.'

A breadth of vocabulary is a key component to successful reading comprehension. Much research has shown that the breadth of children's vocabulary has a direct correlation with children's reading comprehension and future life chances. In 2002, Beck, McKeown & Kucan, identified a lack of targeted vocabulary instruction in schools, although, nowadays, most UK schools have a vocabulary development approach woven throughout their curriculum. *Daily Word Ladders for Fluency* will provide schools with an invaluable resource to supplement their approach to developing vocabulary breadth, whilst also reinforcing and embedding decoding skills.

Regular use of these word ladders as part of a rich and varied language development programme can support children to become familiar with a wider range of words and their definitions. They can also reinforce spelling patterns and exceptions that the children are learning. Furthermore, as children read the words from these ladders in context they are supported to read with automaticity (rapid word reading without conscious decoding). This allows

them to read with prosody (expressive, phrased reading) which supports comprehension. Through this fluent reading, the children's knowledge of literary language grows.

Developing a playfulness with words is a further benefit of word ladders. Word problems can encourage an excitement around language and may help train concentration. This, in turn, can encourage further interaction and longer periods of concentration. It is well known that succeeding in solving tricky problems helps to develop confidence and boost self-esteem. Success may then lead to increased acceptance of challenges in other areas of learning. Development of vocabulary also supports an increasing knowledge and understanding of the world. In addition, if children work collaboratively on these ladders, they can be taught to build social and oracy skills and learn to take turns when listening to one another. Aside from practical considerations, vocabulary development can also allow children to appreciate the beauty of our language.

Herts for Learning (HfL) recognises the need to support children who can decode but struggle to understand what they read. The *HfL Reading Fluency Project* was founded on the question: if a child reads a text with expert prosody, can that lead to better understanding? Automatic word recognition is intrinsic to the success of this programme, as automaticity when reading supports an appropriate reading rate which is a crucial element for comprehension. Regular engagement with meaningful language play, such as through word ladder activities, ensures that vocabulary breadth and automatised decoding are developed hand in hand. As such, HfL recognises the word ladders as a useful tool to achieving the aims as outlined in the National Curriculum.

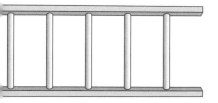
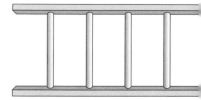

How to use

In this book you'll find 84 mini word study lessons that are also child-pleasing games! To complete each word ladder takes just ten minutes but actively involves each learner in analysing the structure and meaning of words. To play, children begin with one word and then make a series of other words by changing or rearranging the letters in the word before. With regular use, word ladders can go a long way towards developing your children's decoding and vocabulary skills.

How do word ladders work?

Let's say our first word ladder begins with the word *walk*. The instructions will tell children to change one letter in *walk* to make a word that means 'to speak'. The word children will make is *talk*. The next word will then ask children to make a change in *talk* to form another word – perhaps *chalk* or *tall*. At the top of the ladder, children will have a final word that is in some way related to the first word – for example, *run*. If children get stuck on a rung along the way, they can come back to it, because the words before and after will give them the clues they need to go on.

How do word ladders benefit children?

Word ladders are great for building children's decoding, phonics, spelling and vocabulary skills. When children add or rearrange letters to make a new word from one they have just made, they must examine sound–symbol relationships closely. This is just the kind of analysis that all children need to perform in order to learn how to decode and spell accurately. And when the puzzle adds a bit of meaning in the form of a definition

(for example, 'Make a word that means to say something'), it helps extend children's understanding of words and concepts. All of these skills are key to children's success in learning to read and write. So even though the word ladders will feel like a game, your children will be practising essential literacy skills at the same time!

How do I teach a word ladder lesson?

Word ladders are incredibly easy and quick to implement. Here are four simple steps:

1. Choose one of the 84 word ladders to try. (The first four pages feature easier ladders; you may want to start with those.)

2. Make a copy of the word ladder for each child.

3. Choose whether you want to do your word ladders with the class as a whole, or for children to work alone, in pairs, or in groups. (You might do the first few together, until children are ready to work more independently.)

4. For each new word, children will see two clues: the kinds of changes they need to make to the previous word ('Rearrange the letters' or 'Add two letters'), and a definition of or clue to the meaning of the word. Sometimes this clue will be a sentence in which the word is used in context but is left out for children to fill in. Move from word to word this way, up the whole word ladder.

That's the lesson in a nutshell! It should take no longer than ten minutes to do. Once you're finished, you may wish to extend the lesson by asking children to sort the words into various categories. This can

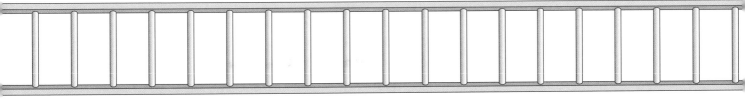

help them deepen their understanding of word relationships. For instance, they could sort them into:

- grammatical categories (Which words are nouns? Verbs?)

- word structure (Which words have a long vowel and which don't? Which contain a consonant blend?)

- word meaning (Which words express what a person can do or feel? Which do not?)

Look for the **bonus boxes** with stars. These are particularly difficult words you may want to pre-teach. Or you can do these ladders as a group so that children will not get stuck on this rung.

About the author

Timothy V. Rasinski is professor of literacy education at Kent State University in Ohio. He began his career as a classroom teacher. Since then, he's written and edited more than 50 books and 200 articles on reading education, including the best-selling *Megabook of Fluency* and the seminal *The Fluent Reader*.

In 2020, the International Literacy Association awarded Tim the William S. Gray Citation of Merit honour. This award honours a nationally or internationally known individual for their outstanding contributions to the field of reading/ literacy. Of Tim, the International Literacy Association said 'Tim Rasinski is one of those names that's synonymous with high-quality literacy research, resources and professional development, especially when it comes to foundational reading and writing skills and struggling readers.'

Tips for working with word ladders

- List all the 'answers' for the ladder (that is, the words for each rung) in random order on the whiteboard. Ask children to choose words from the list to complete the puzzle.

- Add your own clues to give children extra help as they work through each rung of a ladder. A recent event in your classroom or community could even inspire clues for words.

- If children are stuck on a particular rung, say the word aloud and see if children can spell it correctly by making appropriate changes in the previous word. Elaborate on the meanings of the words as children move their way up the ladder.

- Challenge children to come up with alternative definitions for the same words. Many words, like bat, pet, bill and lot, have multiple meanings.

- Once children complete a ladder, add the words to a word wall. Encourage children to use the words in their speaking and writing.

Farm fun

Read the clues, then write the words.
Start at the bottom and climb to the top.

Farm animal with a snout and curly tail.
Change the last letter.

A deep hole in the ground.
Change the vowel.

5 — — —

4 — — —

An animal that lives with a person.
Change the vowel.

3 — — —

A pan used for cooking.
'Dad makes soup in a big ___.'
Change the first letter.

2 — — —

A bed for a baby.
Change the last letter.

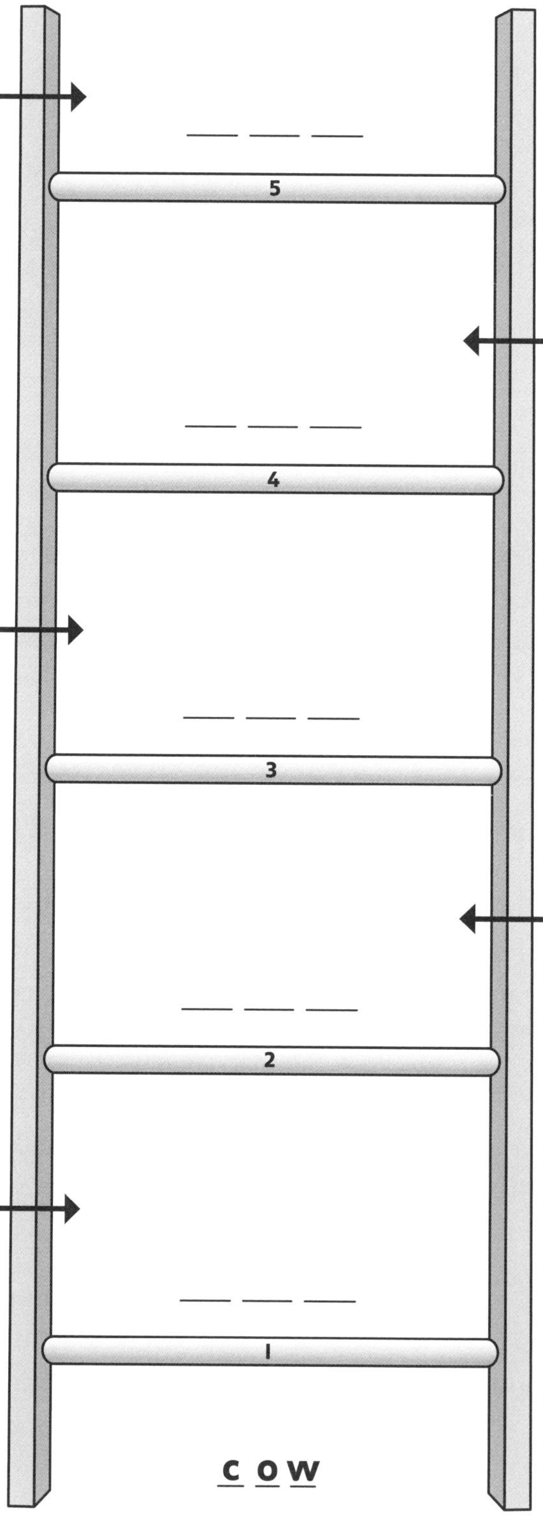

1 — — —

c o w

Daily Word Ladders for Fluency   **SCHOLASTIC**

Dinner's ready

Read the clues, then write the words.
Start at the bottom and climb to the top.

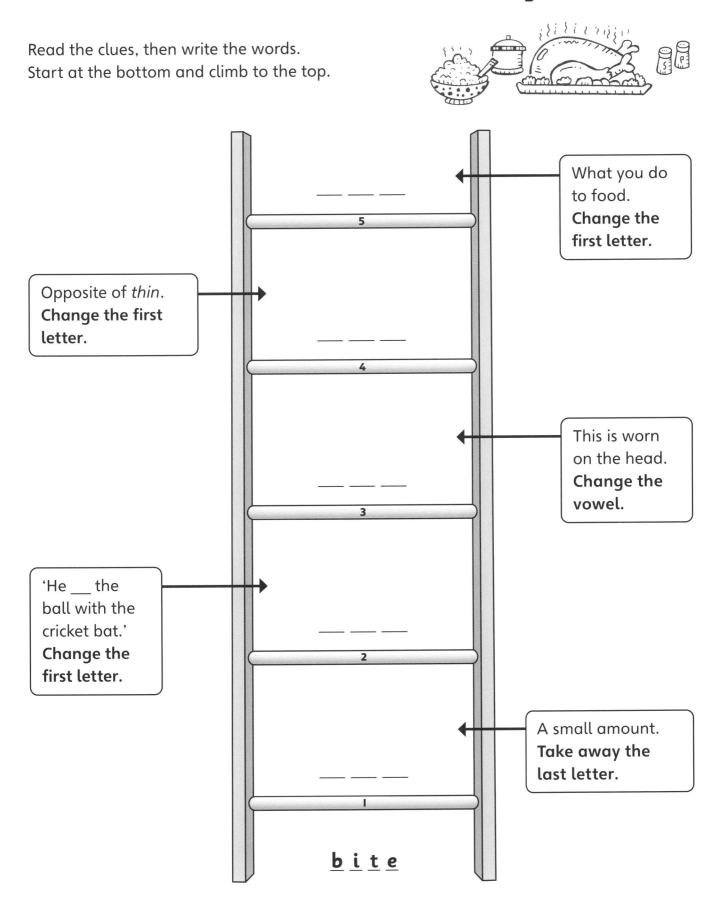

5 ___ ___ ___ ___

What you do to food. **Change the first letter.**

Opposite of *thin*. **Change the first letter.**

4 ___ ___ ___ ___

This is worn on the head. **Change the vowel.**

3 ___ ___ ___

'He ___ the ball with the cricket bat.' **Change the first letter.**

2 ___ ___ ___

A small amount. **Take away the last letter.**

1

<u>b</u> <u>i</u> <u>t</u> <u>e</u>

Inside out

Read the clues, then write the words.
Start at the bottom and climb to the top.

Opposite of *in*.
Change the first letter.

→ __ __ __

6

← You use scissors to do this.
Change the vowel.

__ __ __

5

An animal that has kittens.
Change the first letter.

→ __ __ __

4

← A pig is short and ___.
Change the last letter.

__ __ __

3

This blows air.
Change the vowel.

→ __ __ __

2

← Part of a fish.
Add one letter to the beginning.

__ __ __

1

i n

Daily Word Ladders for Fluency **■SCHOLASTIC**

Name _____

Around the clock

Read the clues, then write the words.
Start at the bottom and climb to the top.

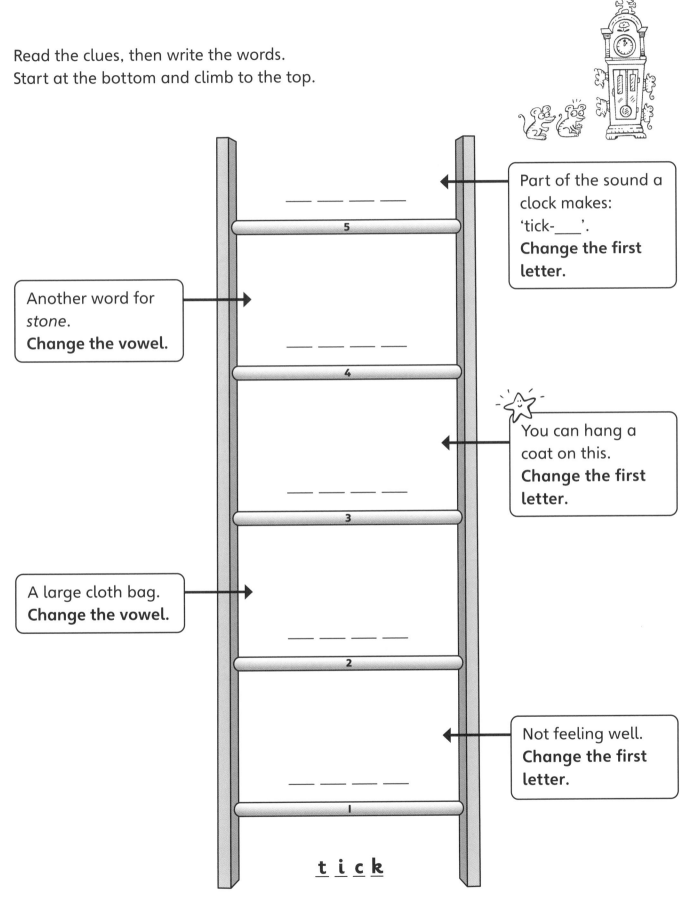

Part of the sound a clock makes: 'tick-___'.
Change the first letter.

Another word for *stone*.
Change the vowel.

You can hang a coat on this.
Change the first letter.

A large cloth bag.
Change the vowel.

Not feeling well.
Change the first letter.

t i c k

Name _____

Animal enemies

Read the clues, then write the words.
Start at the bottom and climb to the top.

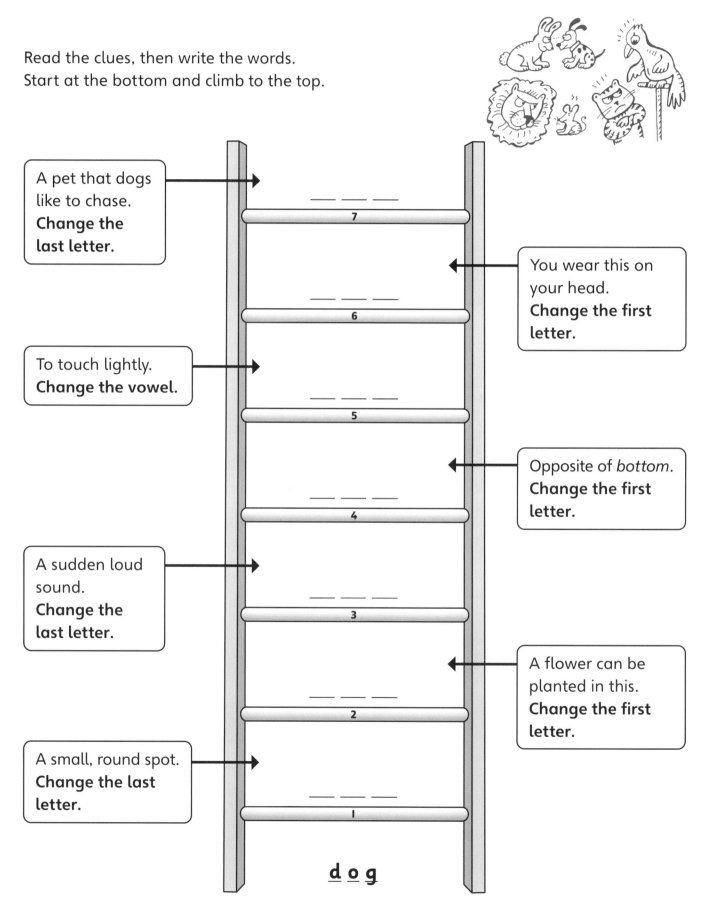

A pet that dogs like to chase. **Change the last letter.**

— — — —
7

You wear this on your head. **Change the first letter.**

— — — —
6

To touch lightly. **Change the vowel.**

— — — —
5

Opposite of *bottom*. **Change the first letter.**

— — — —
4

A sudden loud sound. **Change the last letter.**

— — — —
3

A flower can be planted in this. **Change the first letter.**

— — — —
2

A small, round spot. **Change the last letter.**

— — — —
1

<u>d o g</u>

Daily Word Ladders for Fluency **SCHOLASTIC**

Air travel

Read the clues, then write the words.
Start at the bottom and climb to the top.

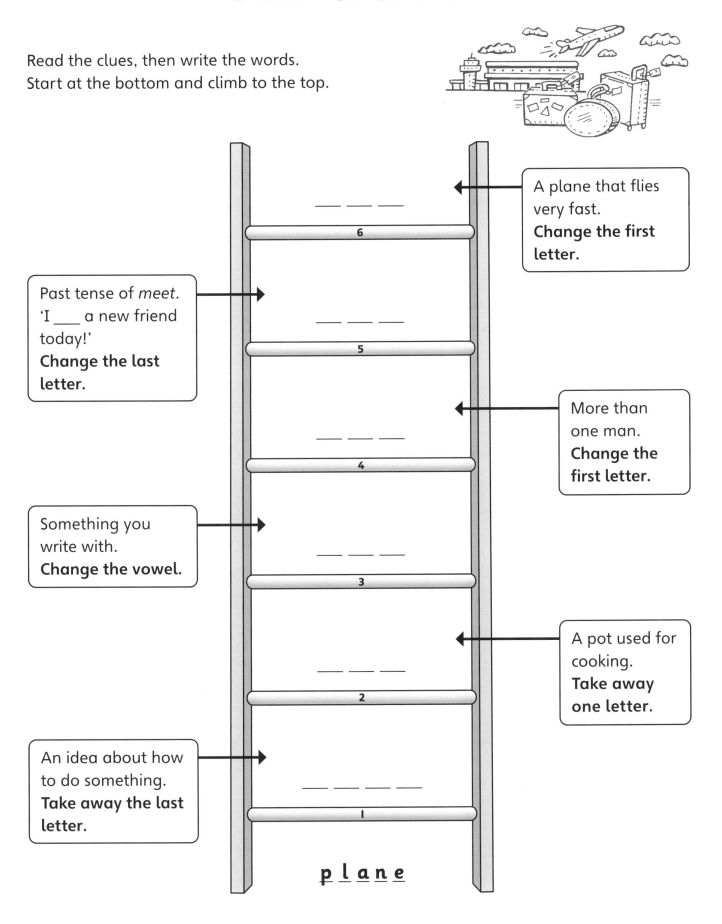

A plane that flies very fast. **Change the first letter.**

Past tense of *meet*. 'I ___ a new friend today!' **Change the last letter.**

More than one man. **Change the first letter.**

Something you write with. **Change the vowel.**

A pot used for cooking. **Take away one letter.**

An idea about how to do something. **Take away the last letter.**

6

5

4

3

2

1

p l a n e

Name _____

Opposites attract

Read the clues, then write the words.
Start at the bottom and climb to the top.

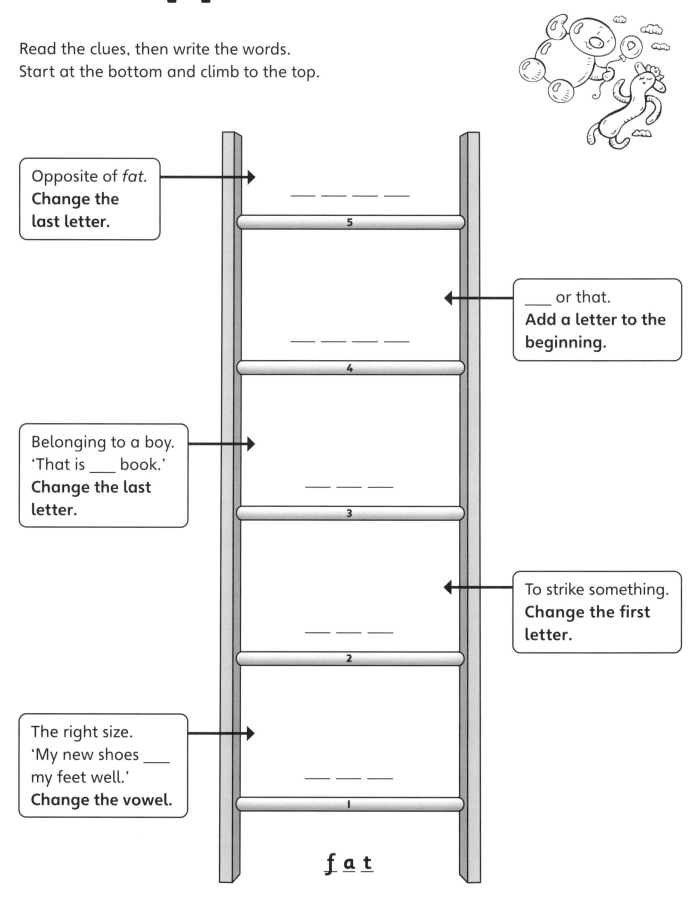

Opposite of *fat.*
Change the last letter.

— — — — —

5

___ or that.
Add a letter to the beginning.

— — — —

4

Belonging to a boy.
'That is ___ book.'
Change the last letter.

— — —

3

To strike something.
Change the first letter.

— — —

2

The right size.
'My new shoes ___ my feet well.'
Change the vowel.

— — —

1

f a t

Daily Word Ladders for Fluency **SCHOLASTIC**

Name _____

Get well soon

Read the clues, then write the words.
Start at the bottom and climb to the top.

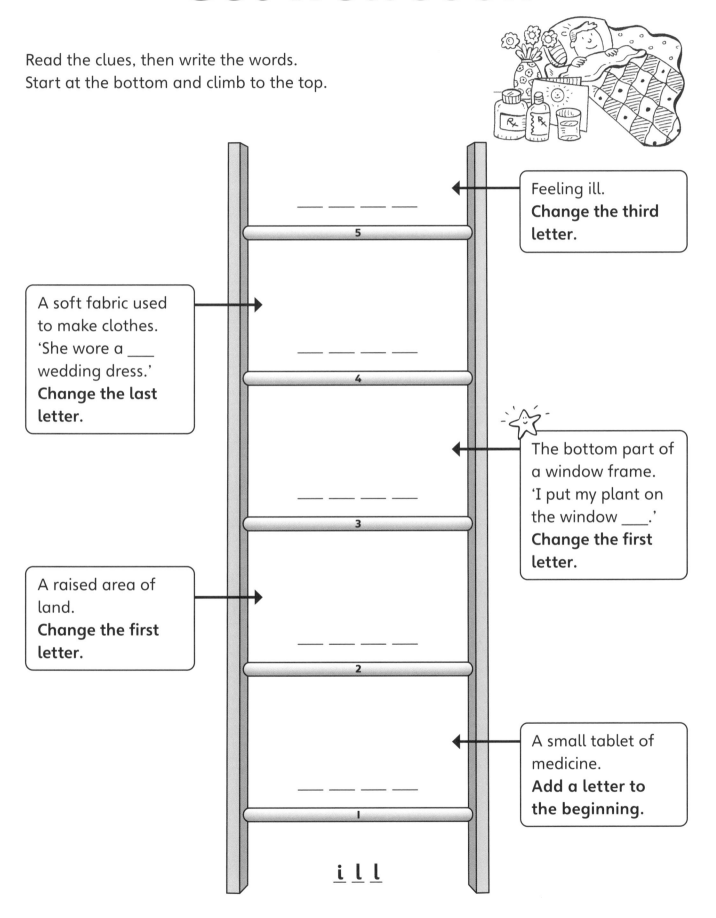

Feeling ill.
Change the third letter.

5 _ _ _ _

A soft fabric used to make clothes. 'She wore a ___ wedding dress.' **Change the last letter.**

4 _ _ _ _

The bottom part of a window frame. 'I put my plant on the window ___.' **Change the first letter.**

3 _ _ _ _

A raised area of land. **Change the first letter.**

2 _ _ _ _

A small tablet of medicine. **Add a letter to the beginning.**

1 _ _ _ _

i l l

Give a dog a bone

Read the clues, then write the words.
Start at the bottom and climb to the top.

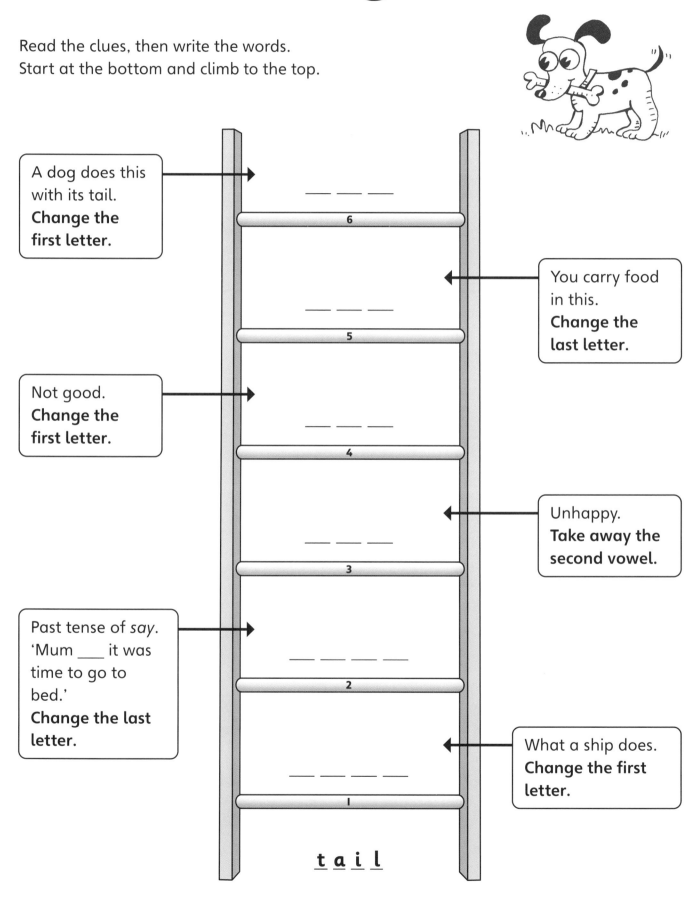

A dog does this with its tail. **Change the first letter.**

_ _ _

6

You carry food in this. **Change the last letter.**

_ _ _ _

5

Not good. **Change the first letter.**

_ _ _

4

Unhappy. **Take away the second vowel.**

_ _ _ _

3

Past tense of *say*. 'Mum ___ it was time to go to bed.' **Change the last letter.**

_ _ _ _

2

What a ship does. **Change the first letter.**

_ _ _ _

1

<u>t a i l</u>

Name _____

Here to there

Read the clues, then write the words.
Start at the bottom and climb to the top.

5 — — — —

Moving much faster than a walk.
Change the first letter.

Enjoyment in doing something.
'We have ___ dancing to the music.'
Take away the last two letters, then add one.

4 — — —

To hold as much as possible.
'The pot is ___ of water.'
Change the vowel.

3 — — — —

To drop to the ground.
'I saw him ___ off the chair.'
Change the first letter.

2 — — — —

This stands between two rooms.
Change the last letter.

1 — — — —

w a l k

Name _____

Take a seat

Read the clues, then write the words.
Start at the bottom and climb to the top.

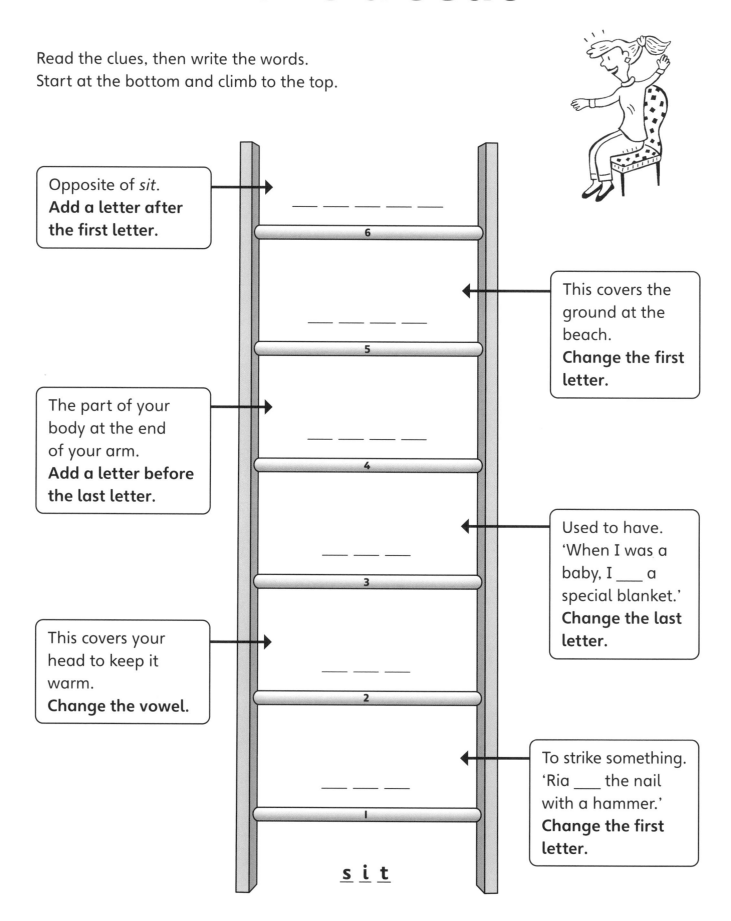

Opposite of *sit*.
Add a letter after the first letter.

This covers the ground at the beach.
Change the first letter.

The part of your body at the end of your arm.
Add a letter before the last letter.

Used to have. 'When I was a baby, I ___ a special blanket.'
Change the last letter.

This covers your head to keep it warm.
Change the vowel.

To strike something. 'Ria ___ the nail with a hammer.'
Change the first letter.

6 _ _ _ _ _ _

5 _ _ _ _ _

4 _ _ _ _ _

3 _ _ _ _

2 _ _ _

1 _ _ _

<u>s</u> <u>i</u> <u>t</u>

Daily Word Ladders for Fluency **■SCHOLASTIC**

Name _____

Fur facts

Read the clues, then write the words.
Start at the bottom and climb to the top.

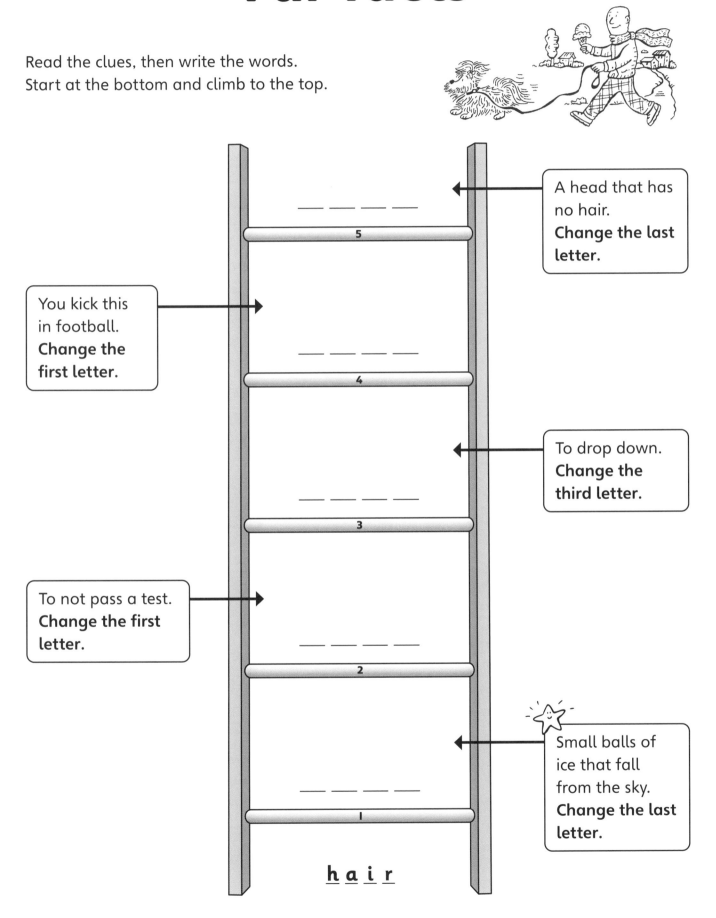

_ _ _ _ _ (5)

A head that has no hair. **Change the last letter.**

You kick this in football. **Change the first letter.**

_ _ _ _ _ (4)

To drop down. **Change the third letter.**

_ _ _ _ _ (3)

To not pass a test. **Change the first letter.**

_ _ _ _ _ (2)

Small balls of ice that fall from the sky. **Change the last letter.**

_ _ _ _ _ (1)

<u>h</u> <u>a</u> <u>i</u> <u>r</u>

Shipshape

Read the clues, then write the words.
Start at the bottom and climb to the top.

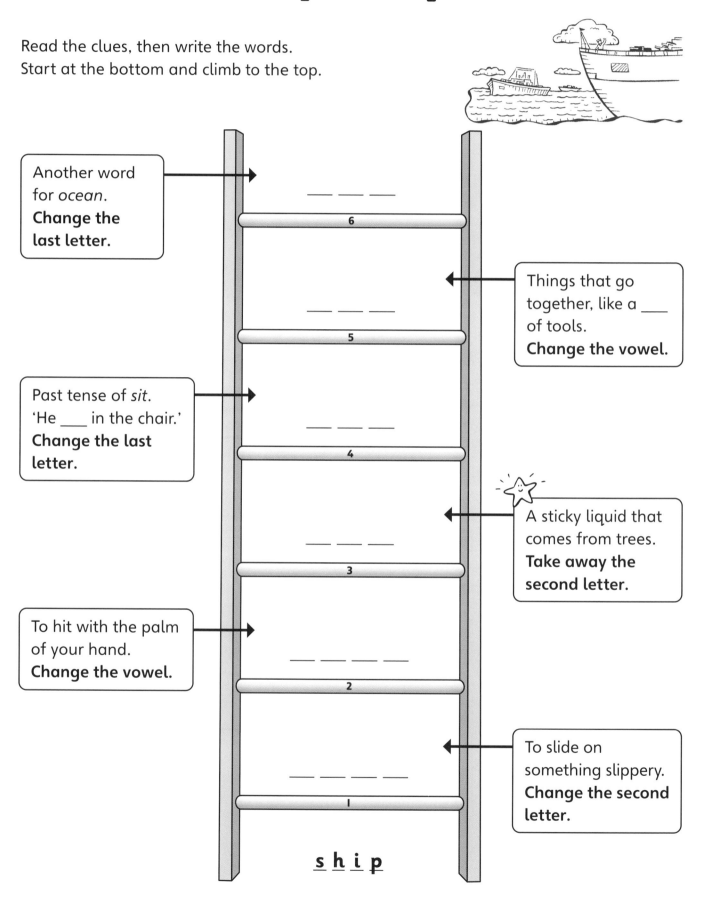

Another word for *ocean*.
Change the last letter.

— — —
6

— — —
5

Things that go together, like a ___ of tools.
Change the vowel.

Past tense of *sit*.
'He ___ in the chair.'
Change the last letter.

— — —
4

— — —
3

A sticky liquid that comes from trees.
Take away the second letter.

To hit with the palm of your hand.
Change the vowel.

— — — —
2

— — — —
1

To slide on something slippery.
Change the second letter.

s h i p

Daily Word Ladders for Fluency **SCHOLASTIC**

Name _____

Fancy footwear

Read the clues, then write the words.
Start at the bottom and climb to the top.

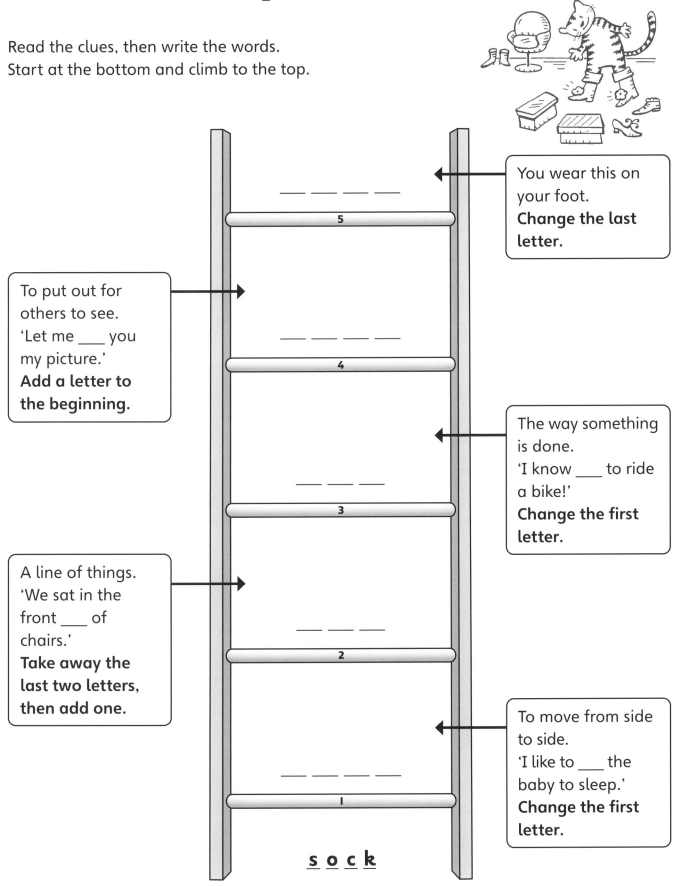

You wear this on your foot.
Change the last letter.

— — — —
5

To put out for others to see.
'Let me ___ you my picture.'
Add a letter to the beginning.

— — — —
4

The way something is done.
'I know ___ to ride a bike!'
Change the first letter.

— — —
3

A line of things.
'We sat in the front ___ of chairs.'
Take away the last two letters, then add one.

— — —
2

To move from side to side.
'I like to ___ the baby to sleep.'
Change the first letter.

— — — —
1

<u>s o c k</u>

Counting up

Read the clues, then write the words.
Start at the bottom and climb to the top.

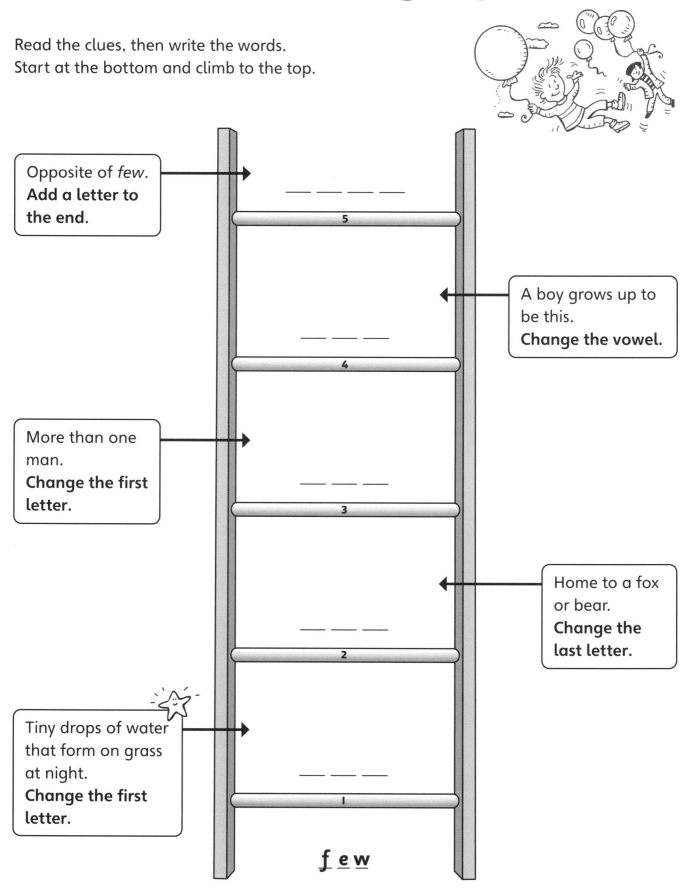

Opposite of *few*.
Add a letter to the end.

— — — — —

5

A boy grows up to be this.
Change the vowel.

— — — —

4

More than one man.
Change the first letter.

— — — —

3

Home to a fox or bear.
Change the last letter.

— — —

2

Tiny drops of water that form on grass at night.
Change the first letter.

— — —

1

f e w

Daily Word Ladders for Fluency **SCHOLASTIC**

Name _____

Personality change

Read the clues, then write the words.
Start at the bottom and climb to the top.

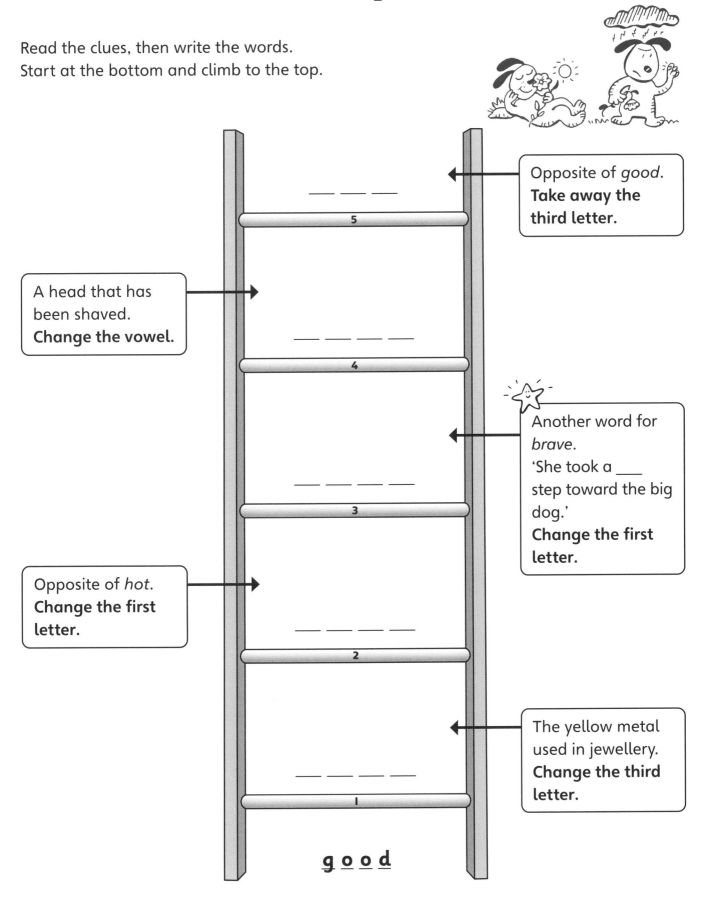

Opposite of *good*.
**Take away the
third letter.**

A head that has
been shaved.
Change the vowel.

5
_ _ _ _

4
_ _ _ _ _

Another word for
brave.
'She took a ___
step toward the big
dog.'
**Change the first
letter.**

Opposite of *hot*.
**Change the first
letter.**

3
_ _ _ _ _

2
_ _ _ _ _

The yellow metal
used in jewellery.
**Change the third
letter.**

1
_ _ _ _

g o o d

Name _____

Frosty fun

Read the clues, then write the words.
Start at the bottom and climb to the top.

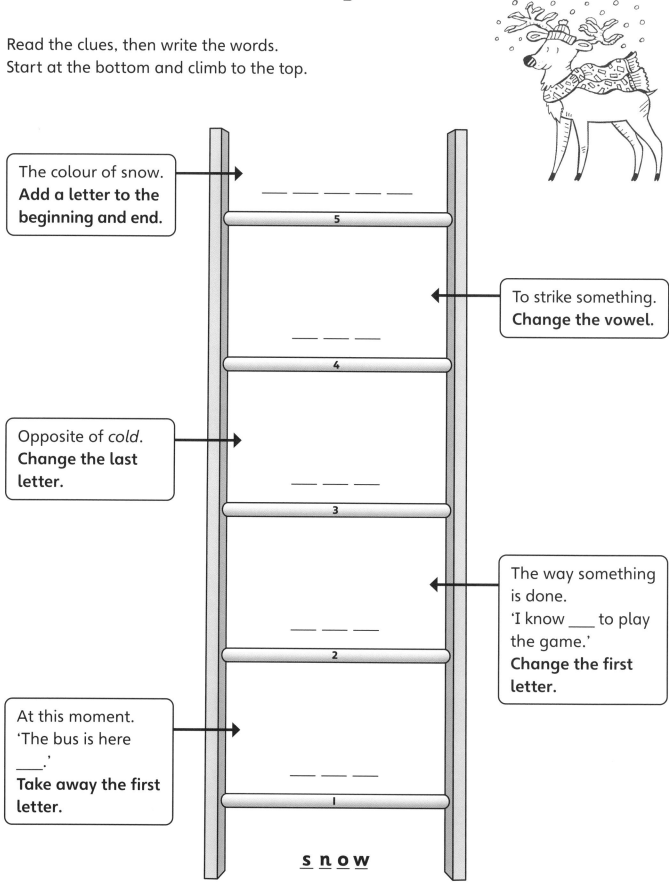

The colour of snow.
Add a letter to the beginning and end.

5 _ _ _ _ _

To strike something.
Change the vowel.

4 _ _ _ _

Opposite of *cold*.
Change the last letter.

3 _ _ _ _

The way something is done.
'I know ___ to play the game.'
Change the first letter.

2 _ _ _ _

At this moment.
'The bus is here ___.'
Take away the first letter.

1 _ _ _ _

s n o w

Daily Word Ladders for Fluency **■SCHOLASTIC**

One more

Read the clues, then write the words.
Start at the bottom and climb to the top.

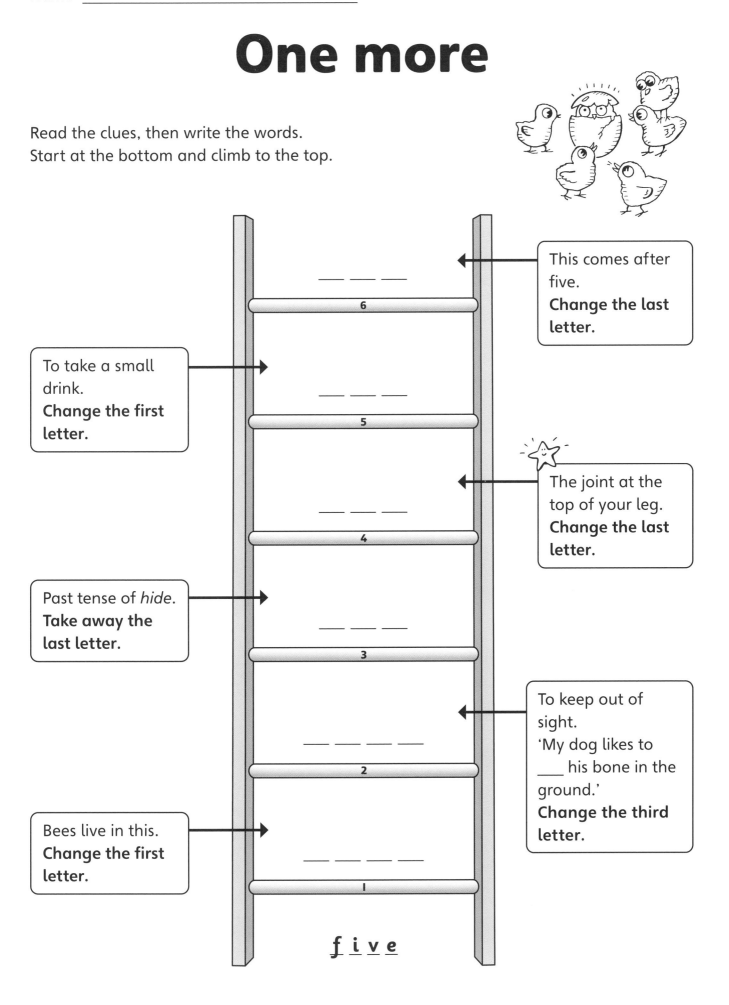

This comes after five.
Change the last letter.

To take a small drink.
Change the first letter.

The joint at the top of your leg.
Change the last letter.

Past tense of *hide*.
Take away the last letter.

To keep out of sight.
'My dog likes to ___ his bone in the ground.'
Change the third letter.

Bees live in this.
Change the first letter.

f i v e

6

5

4

3

2

1

Under the stars

Read the clues, then write the words.
Start at the bottom and climb to the top.

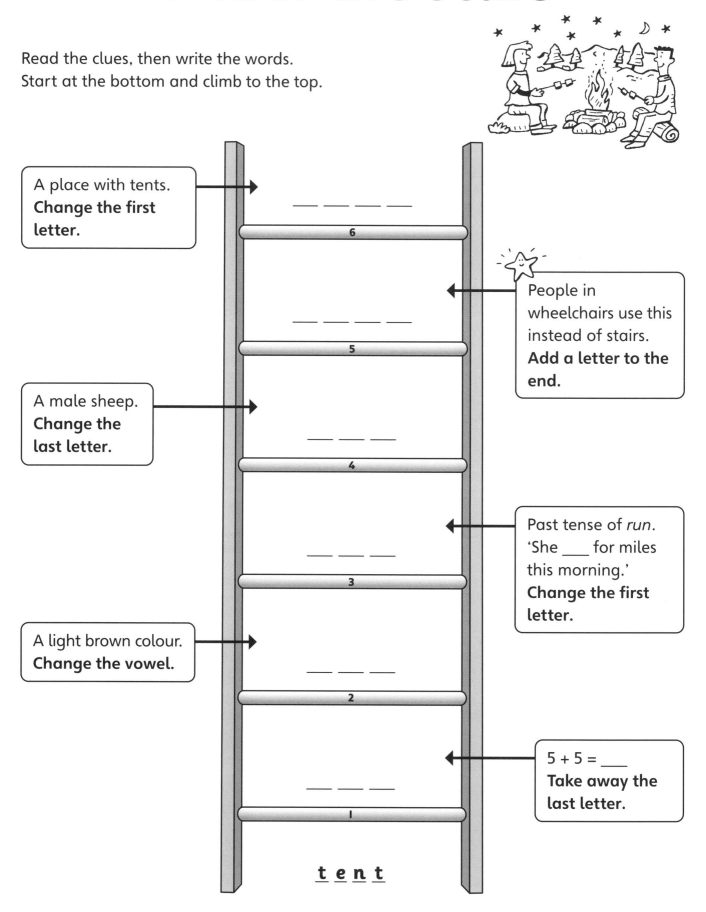

A place with tents.
Change the first letter.

→ 6 __ __ __ __

People in wheelchairs use this instead of stairs.
Add a letter to the end.

← 5 __ __ __ __ __

A male sheep.
Change the last letter.

→ 4 __ __ __

Past tense of *run*.
'She ___ for miles this morning.'
Change the first letter.

← 3 __ __ __

A light brown colour.
Change the vowel.

→ 2 __ __ __

5 + 5 = ___
Take away the last letter.

← 1 __ __ __

t e n t

Name _____

Baby animals

Read the clues, then write the words.
Start at the bottom and climb to the top.

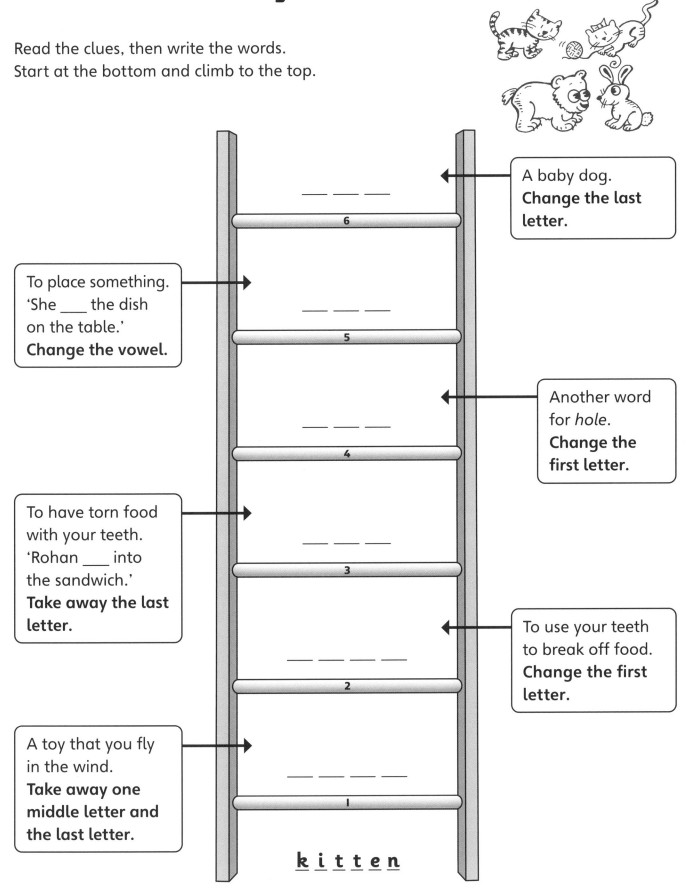

A baby dog.
Change the last letter.

To place something.
'She ___ the dish on the table.'
Change the vowel.

Another word for *hole*.
Change the first letter.

To have torn food with your teeth.
'Rohan ___ into the sandwich.'
Take away the last letter.

To use your teeth to break off food.
Change the first letter.

A toy that you fly in the wind.
Take away one middle letter and the last letter.

6 — — — —

5 — — — —

4 — — — —

3 — — — —

2 — — — —

1 — — — —

k i t t e n

Name _____

Wildlife

Read the clues, then write the words.
Start at the bottom and climb to the top.

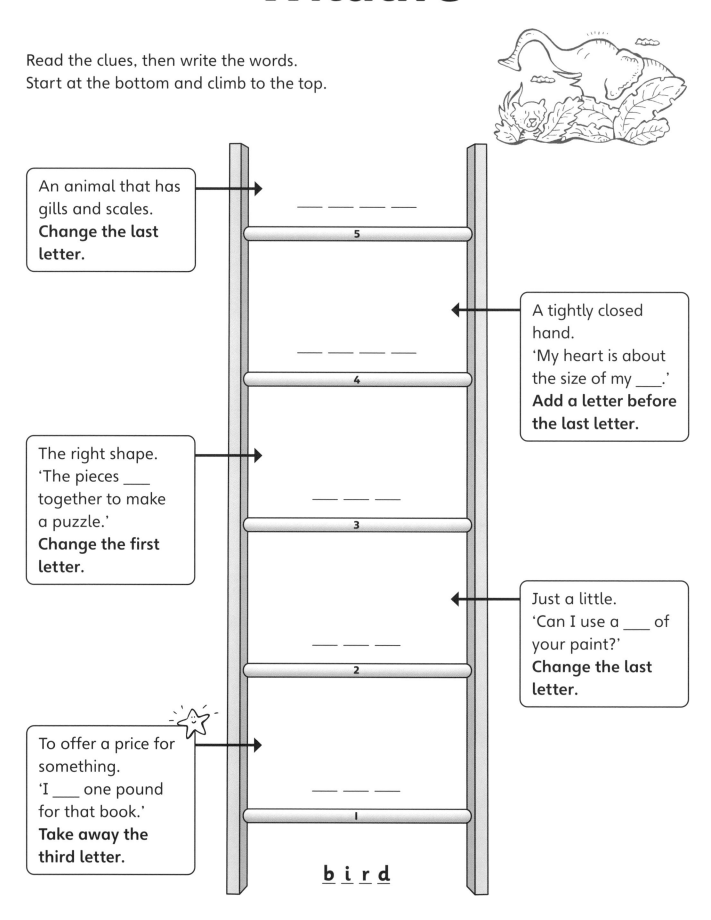

An animal that has gills and scales. **Change the last letter.**

5 _ _ _ _

A tightly closed hand. 'My heart is about the size of my ___.' **Add a letter before the last letter.**

4 _ _ _ _ _

The right shape. 'The pieces ___ together to make a puzzle.' **Change the first letter.**

3 _ _ _ _

Just a little. 'Can I use a ___ of your paint?' **Change the last letter.**

2 _ _ _

To offer a price for something. 'I ___ one pound for that book.' **Take away the third letter.**

1 _ _ _

<u>b</u> <u>i</u> <u>r</u> <u>d</u>

Daily Word Ladders for Fluency **SCHOLASTIC**

Name _____

Raise your voice

Read the clues, then write the words.
Start at the bottom and climb to the top.

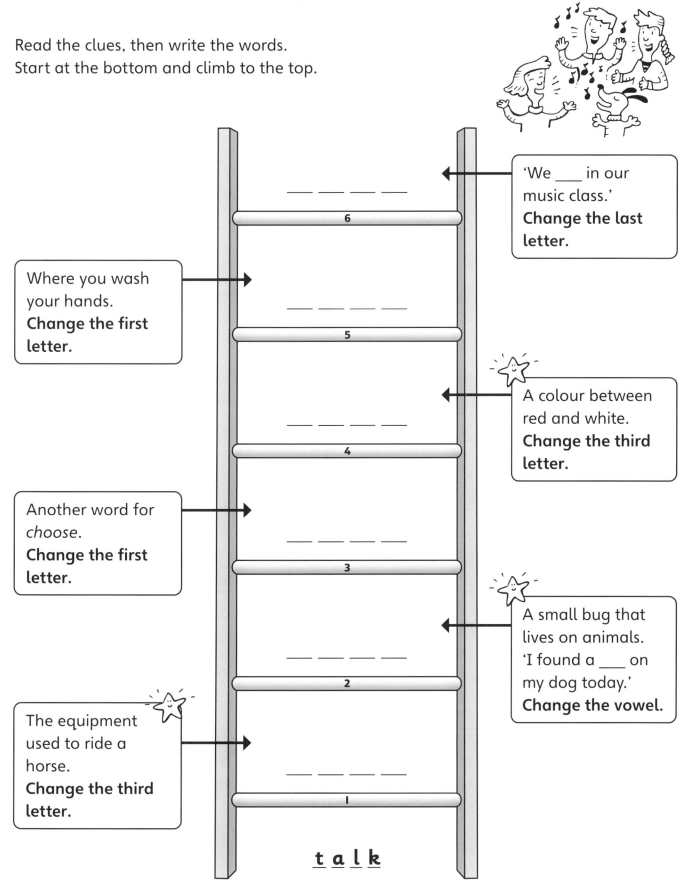

'We ___ in our music class.'
Change the last letter.

Where you wash your hands.
Change the first letter.

6

5

A colour between red and white.
Change the third letter.

4

Another word for *choose.*
Change the first letter.

3

A small bug that lives on animals.
'I found a ___ on my dog today.'
Change the vowel.

2

The equipment used to ride a horse.
Change the third letter.

1

<u>t a l k</u>

Name _____

Winter wear

Read the clues, then write the words.
Start at the bottom and climb to the top.

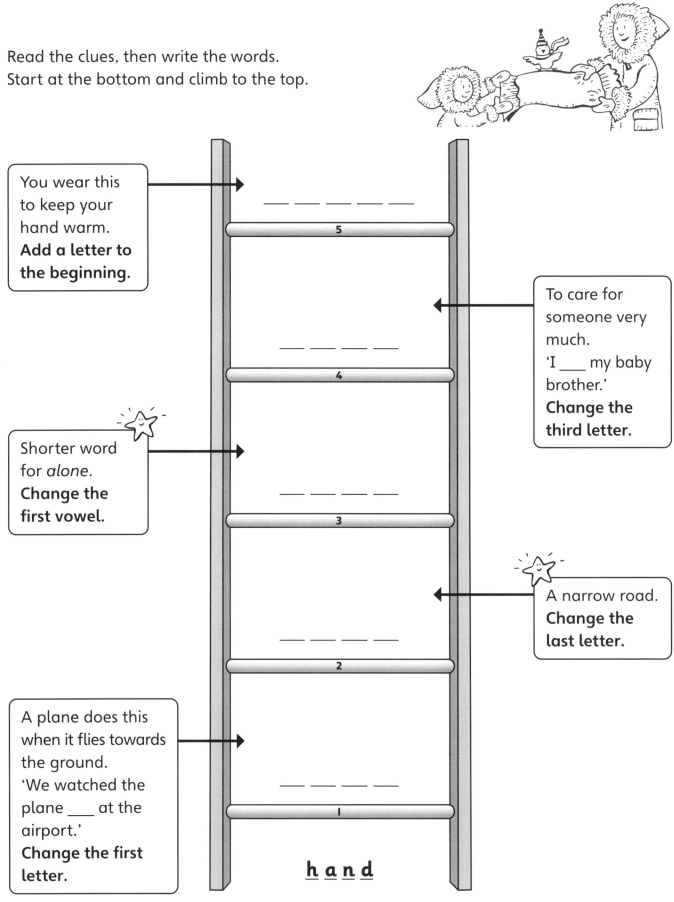

You wear this to keep your hand warm. **Add a letter to the beginning.**

To care for someone very much. 'I ___ my baby brother.' **Change the third letter.**

Shorter word for *alone*. **Change the first vowel.**

A narrow road. **Change the last letter.**

A plane does this when it flies towards the ground. 'We watched the plane ___ at the airport.' **Change the first letter.**

5

4

3

2

1

h a n d

Daily Word Ladders for Fluency **SCHOLASTIC**

Name _____

Candlelight

Read the clues, then write the words.
Start at the bottom and climb to the top.

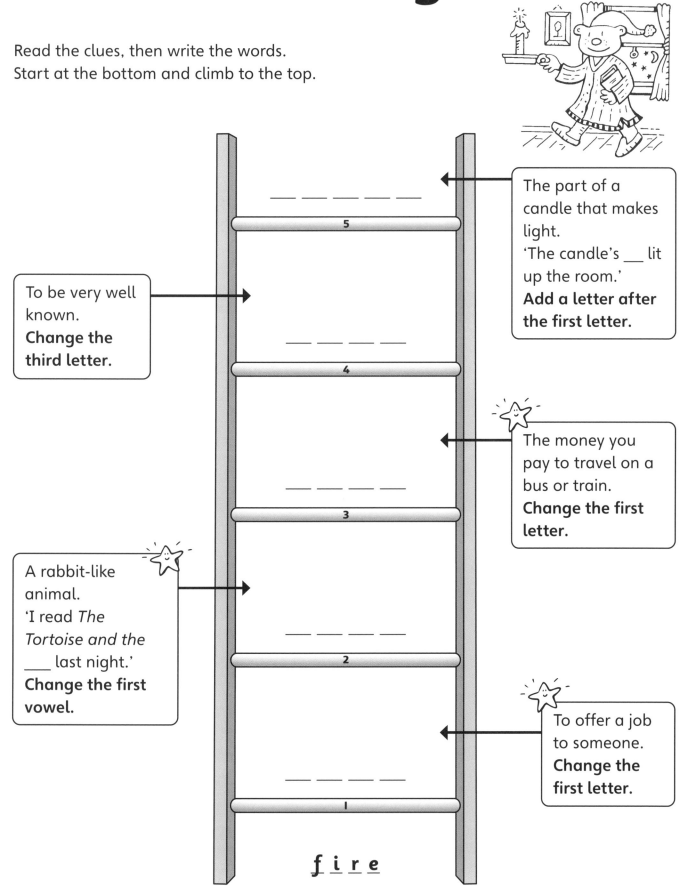

The part of a candle that makes light.
'The candle's ___ lit up the room.'
Add a letter after the first letter.

To be very well known.
Change the third letter.

The money you pay to travel on a bus or train.
Change the first letter.

A rabbit-like animal.
'I read The Tortoise and the ___ last night.'
Change the first vowel.

To offer a job to someone.
Change the first letter.

5 _ _ _ _ _

4 _ _ _ _

3 _ _ _ _

2 _ _ _ _

1 _ _ _ _

f i r e

Name _____

End of the day

Read the clues, then write the words.
Start at the bottom and climb to the top.

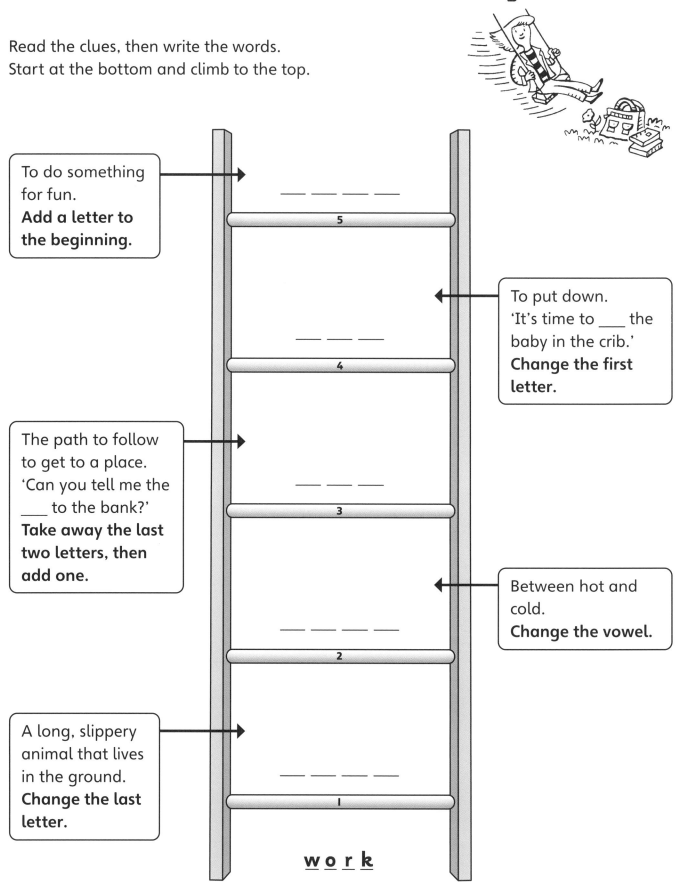

To do something for fun.
Add a letter to the beginning.

— — — —   5

To put down.
'It's time to ___ the baby in the crib.'
Change the first letter.

— — — —   4

The path to follow to get to a place.
'Can you tell me the ___ to the bank?'
Take away the last two letters, then add one.

— — — —   3

Between hot and cold.
Change the vowel.

— — — — —   2

A long, slippery animal that lives in the ground.
Change the last letter.

— — — — —   1

w o r k

Daily Word Ladders for Fluency **SCHOLASTIC**

Finish line

Read the clues, then write the words.
Start at the bottom and climb to the top.

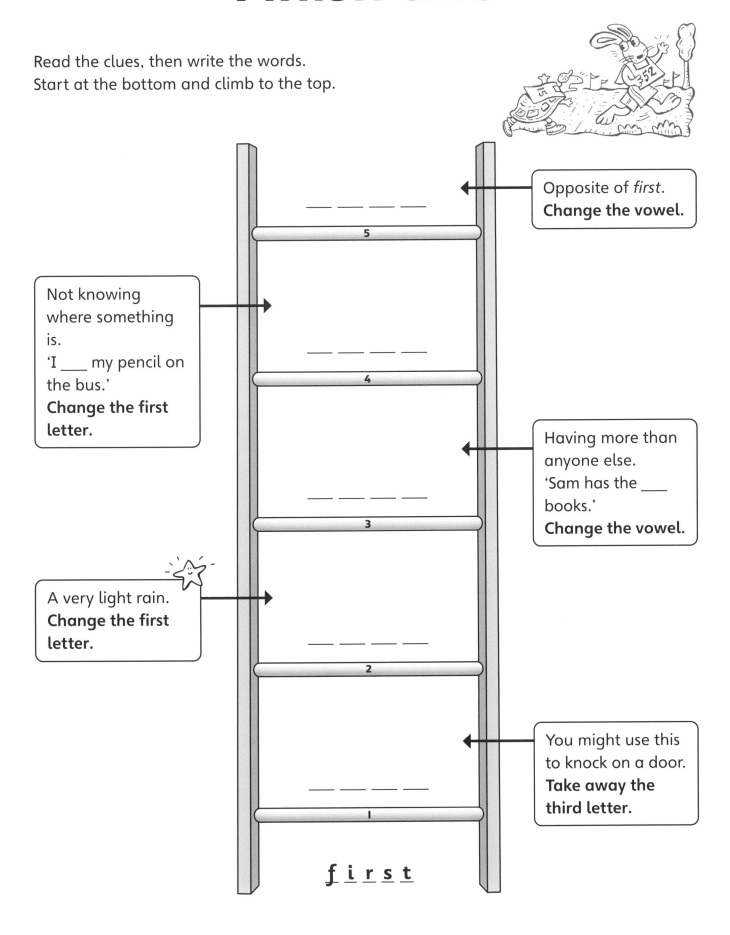

Opposite of *first*.
Change the vowel.

_ _ _ _ _

5

Not knowing where something is.
'I ___ my pencil on the bus.'
Change the first letter.

_ _ _ _ _

4

Having more than anyone else.
'Sam has the ___ books.'
Change the vowel.

_ _ _ _ _

3

A very light rain.
Change the first letter.

_ _ _ _ _

2

You might use this to knock on a door.
Take away the third letter.

_ _ _ _ _

1

f i r s t

Stormy days

Read the clues, then write the words.
Start at the bottom and climb to the top.

'Will you ___ some milk for me, please?'
Change the first letter.

_ _ _ _

6

Comes after three. **Add a vowel before the last letter.**

_ _ _ _

5

'I made this gift just ___ you!'
Change the vowel.

_ _ _

4

Opposite of *near*. **Change the last letter.**

_ _ _

3

A person who really likes a sport.
'My grandpa is a big football ___.'
Change the first letter.

_ _ _

2

To move at a fast speed.
'Yin ___ around the track.'
Take away the second vowel.

_ _ _ _

1

<u>r a i n</u>

Daily Word Ladders for Fluency **SCHOLASTIC**

Climbing limbs

Read the clues, then write the words.
Start at the bottom and climb to the top.

7 — _ _ _ _

You use this for walking. **Change the first letter.**

To keep asking for something. **Change the vowel.**

6 — _ _ _

5 — _ _ _ _

Another word for *insect*. **Change the first letter.**

To put your arms around someone. **Change the last letter.**

4 — _ _ _ _

To sing with your lips closed. **Change the vowel.**

3 — _ _ _

Meat from the leg or shoulder of a pig. **Take away the third letter.**

2 — _ _ _ _

Another word for *hurt*. **Add a letter to the beginning.**

1 — _ _ _ _

<u>a</u> <u>r</u> <u>m</u>

City living

Read the clues, then write the words.
Start at the bottom and climb to the top.

You enter a house through this.
Add two letters to the end.

— — — — —
5

'___ you know how to tie your shoe?'
Take away the last letter.

— —
4

A short name for *Donald*.
Change the first letter.

— — —
3

Opposite of *lost*.
Change the vowel.

— — —
2

To finish a race first. 'I hope I ___ the bicycle race tomorrow.'
Take away the last three letters.

— — —
1

<u>w i n d o w</u>

Daily Word Ladders for Fluency **SCHOLASTIC**

Name _____

The whole story

Read the clues, then write the words.
Start at the bottom and climb to the top.

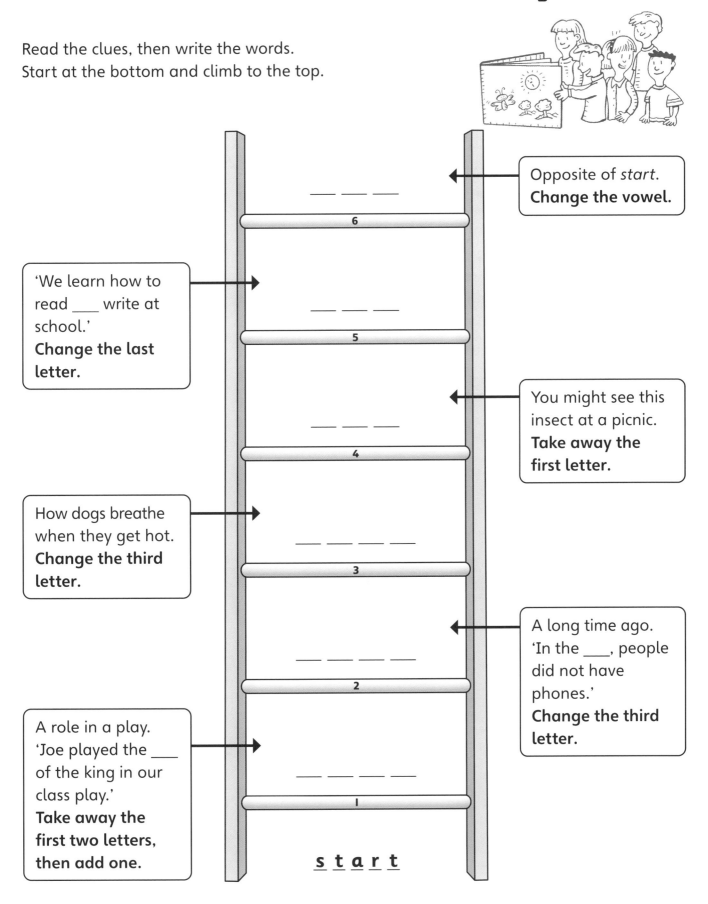

Opposite of *start*.
Change the vowel.

— — — —
6

'We learn how to read ___ write at school.'
Change the last letter.

— — —
5

You might see this insect at a picnic.
Take away the first letter.

— — — —
4

How dogs breathe when they get hot.
Change the third letter.

— — — — —
3

A long time ago. 'In the ___, people did not have phones.'
Change the third letter.

— — — — —
2

A role in a play. 'Joe played the ___ of the king in our class play.'
Take away the first two letters, then add one.

— — — —
1

<u>s t a r t</u>

Let's go fishing

Read the clues, then write the words.
Start at the bottom and climb to the top.

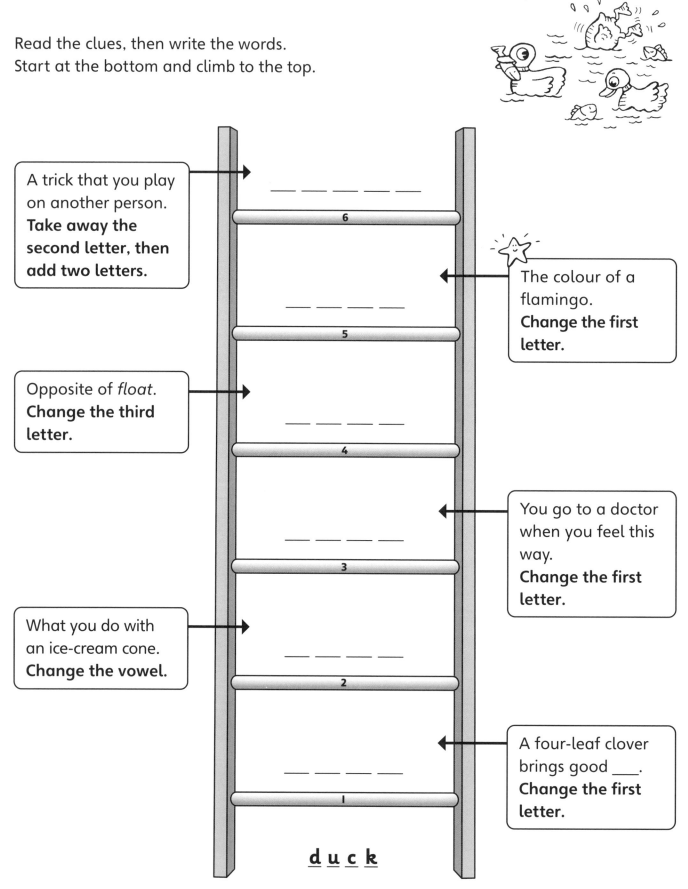

A trick that you play on another person. **Take away the second letter, then add two letters.**

→ _ _ _ _ _ _

6

The colour of a flamingo. **Change the first letter.** ←

_ _ _ _ _

5

Opposite of *float*. **Change the third letter.** →

_ _ _ _ _

4

You go to a doctor when you feel this way. **Change the first letter.** ←

_ _ _ _

3

What you do with an ice-cream cone. **Change the vowel.** →

_ _ _ _

2

A four-leaf clover brings good ___. **Change the first letter.** ←

_ _ _ _ _

1

<u>d u c k</u>

Name _____

Blast off!

Read the clues, then write the words.
Start at the bottom and climb to the top.

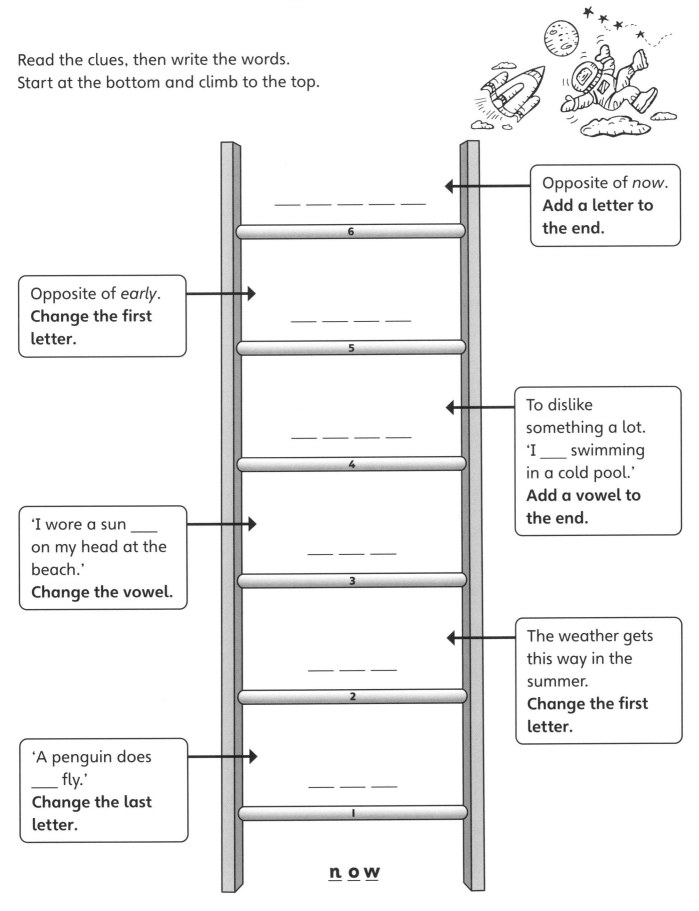

Opposite of *now*.
Add a letter to the end.

6 _____

Opposite of *early*.
Change the first letter.

5 _____

To dislike something a lot.
'I ___ swimming in a cold pool.'
Add a vowel to the end.

4 _____

'I wore a sun ___ on my head at the beach.'
Change the vowel.

3 _____

The weather gets this way in the summer.
Change the first letter.

2 _____

'A penguin does ___ fly.'
Change the last letter.

1 _____

n o w

Name _____

Feathered friends

Read the clues, then write the words.
Start at the bottom and climb to the top.

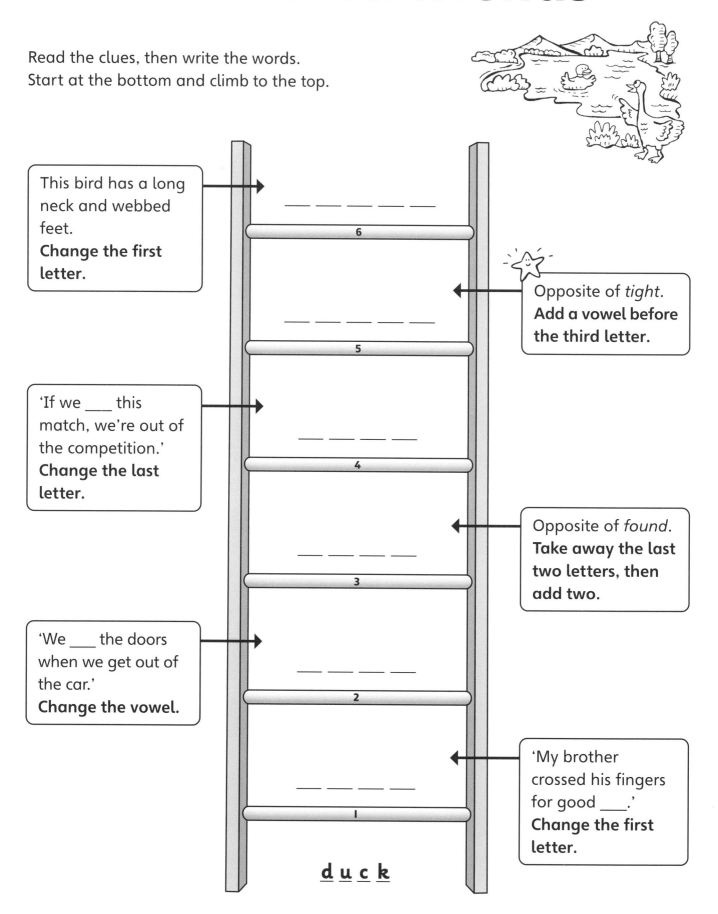

This bird has a long neck and webbed feet. **Change the first letter.**

Opposite of *tight*. **Add a vowel before the third letter.**

'If we ___ this match, we're out of the competition.' **Change the last letter.**

Opposite of *found*. **Take away the last two letters, then add two.**

'We ___ the doors when we get out of the car.' **Change the vowel.**

'My brother crossed his fingers for good ___.' **Change the first letter.**

6

5

4

3

2

1

d u c k

Daily Word Ladders for Fluency **SCHOLASTIC**

Name _____

In the attic

Read the clues, then write the words.
Start at the bottom and climb to the top.

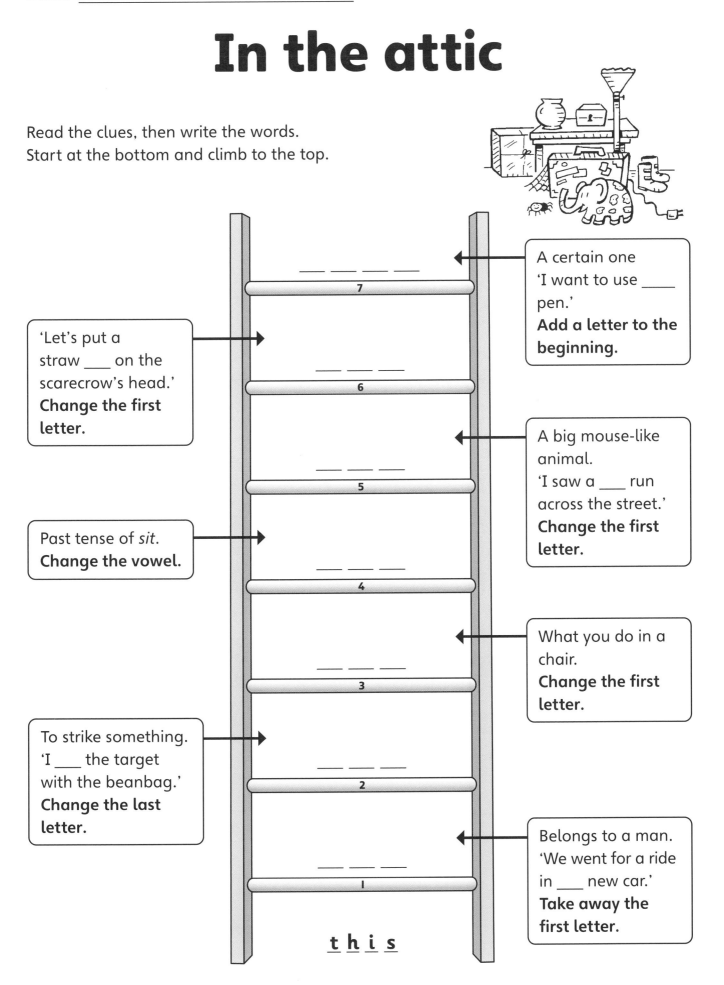

7 — — — — —

A certain one
'I want to use ____ pen.'
Add a letter to the beginning.

'Let's put a straw ___ on the scarecrow's head.'
Change the first letter.

6 — — — —

5 — — — —

A big mouse-like animal.
'I saw a ___ run across the street.'
Change the first letter.

Past tense of *sit*.
Change the vowel.

4 — — — —

What you do in a chair.
Change the first letter.

3 — — — —

To strike something.
'I ___ the target with the beanbag.'
Change the last letter.

2 — — — —

Belongs to a man.
'We went for a ride in ___ new car.'
Take away the first letter.

1 — — — —

<u>t h i s</u>

Utensils

Read the clues, then write the words.
Start at the bottom and climb to the top.

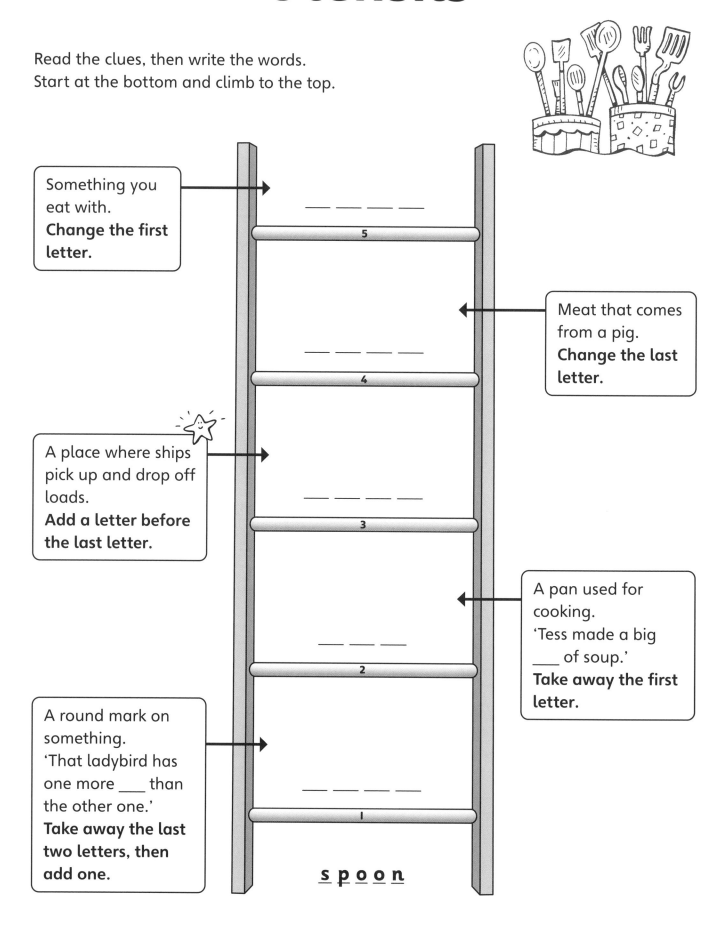

Something you eat with.
Change the first letter.

_ _ _ _ _

5

Meat that comes from a pig.
Change the last letter.

_ _ _ _

4

A place where ships pick up and drop off loads.
Add a letter before the last letter.

_ _ _ _ _

3

A pan used for cooking.
'Tess made a big ___ of soup.'
Take away the first letter.

_ _ _

2

A round mark on something.
'That ladybird has one more ___ than the other one.'
Take away the last two letters, then add one.

_ _ _ _

1

s p o o n

Photocopiable

Daily Word Ladders for Fluency **SCHOLASTIC**

Happy birthday

Read the clues, then write the words.
Start at the bottom and climb to the top.

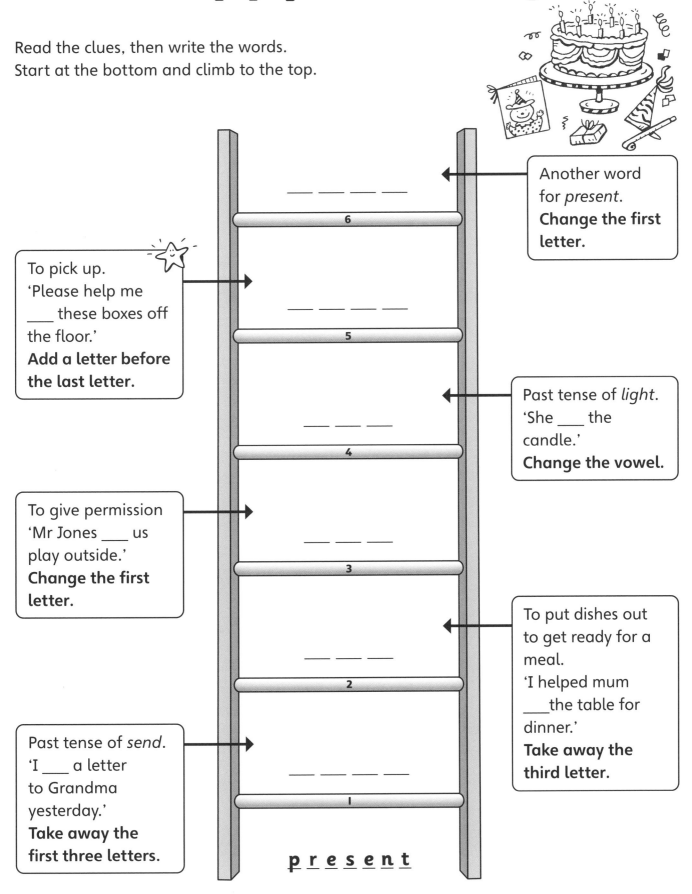

Another word for *present*.
Change the first letter.

____ ____ ____ ____
6

To pick up.
'Please help me ___ these boxes off the floor.'
Add a letter before the last letter.

____ ____ ____ ____ ____
5

Past tense of *light*.
'She ___ the candle.'
Change the vowel.

____ ____ ____ ____
4

To give permission
'Mr Jones ___ us play outside.'
Change the first letter.

____ ____ ____
3

To put dishes out to get ready for a meal.
'I helped mum ___ the table for dinner.'
Take away the third letter.

____ ____ ____ ____
2

Past tense of *send*.
'I ___ a letter to Grandma yesterday.'
Take away the first three letters.

____ ____ ____ ____
1

p r e s e n t

Name _____

New and not-so-new

Read the clues, then write the words.
Start at the bottom and climb to the top.

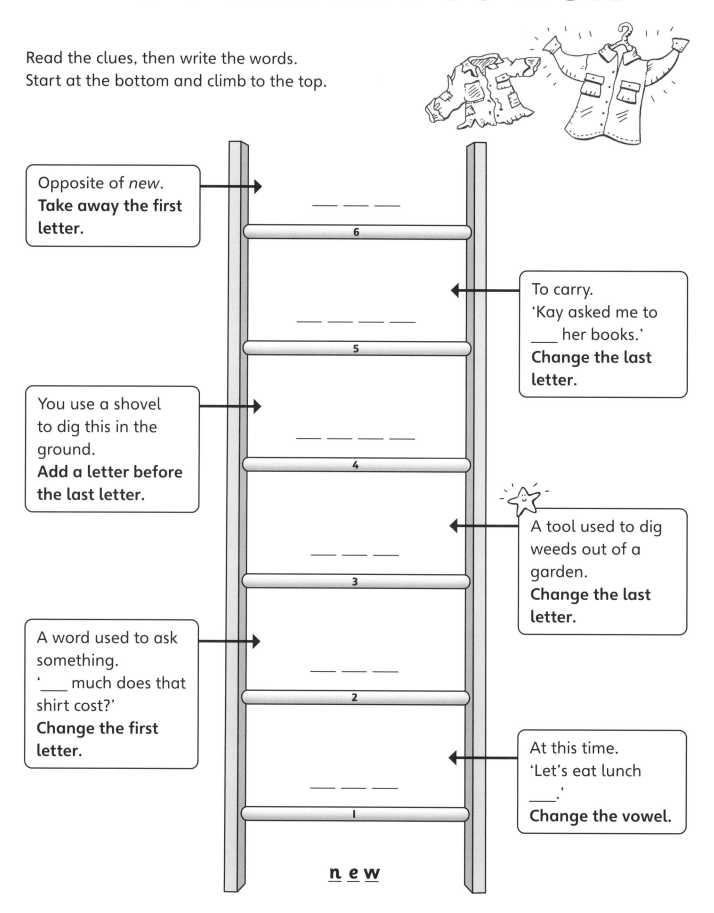

Opposite of *new*.
Take away the first letter.

To carry.
'Kay asked me to ___ her books.'
Change the last letter.

You use a shovel to dig this in the ground.
Add a letter before the last letter.

A tool used to dig weeds out of a garden.
Change the last letter.

A word used to ask something.
'___ much does that shirt cost?'
Change the first letter.

At this time.
'Let's eat lunch ___.'
Change the vowel.

6

5

4

3

2

1

n e w

Daily Word Ladders for Fluency **SCHOLASTIC**

Name _____

In the water

Read the clues, then write the words.
Start at the bottom and climb to the top.

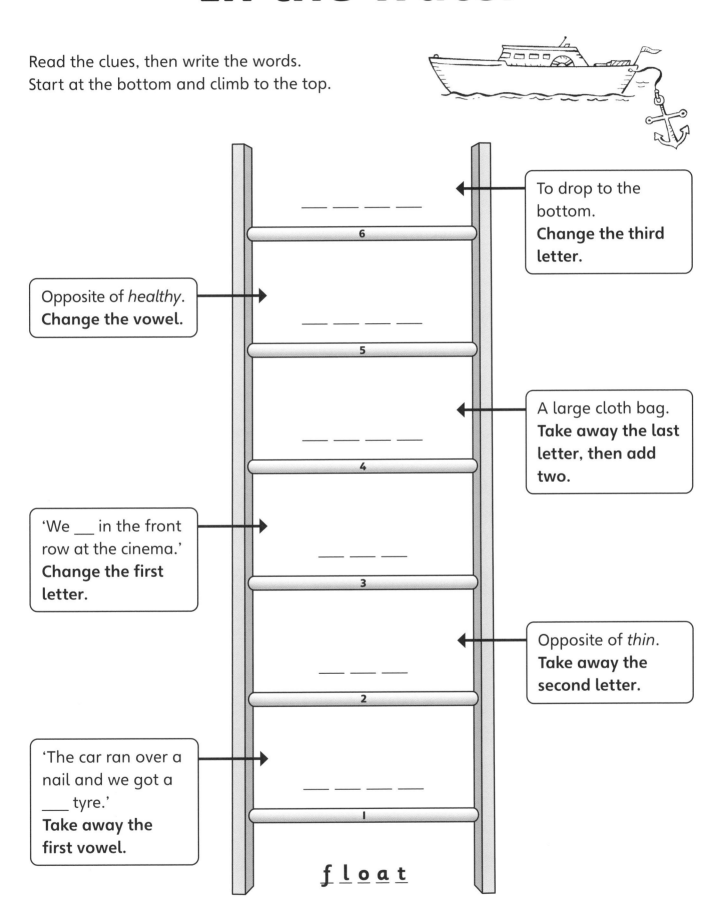

To drop to the bottom.
Change the third letter.

Opposite of *healthy*.
Change the vowel.

A large cloth bag.
Take away the last letter, then add two.

'We ___ in the front row at the cinema.'
Change the first letter.

Opposite of *thin*.
Take away the second letter.

'The car ran over a nail and we got a ___ tyre.'
Take away the first vowel.

6

5

4

3

2

1

f l o a t

Quick wit

Read the clues, then write the words.
Start at the bottom and climb to the top.

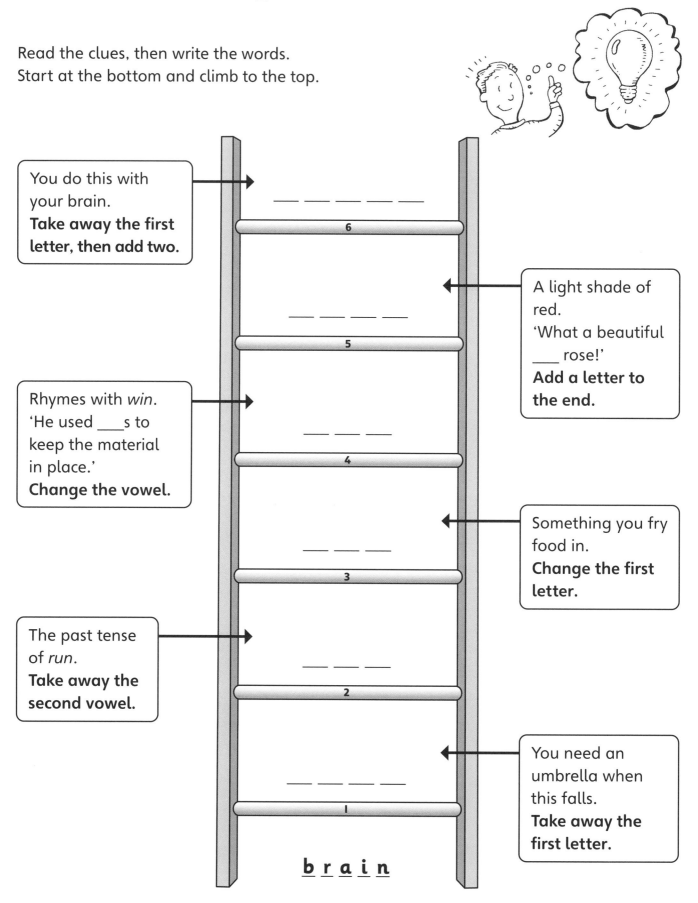

You do this with your brain.
Take away the first letter, then add two.

6 — — — — — —

A light shade of red.
'What a beautiful ___ rose!'
Add a letter to the end.

5 — — — — —

Rhymes with *win*.
'He used ___s to keep the material in place.'
Change the vowel.

4 — — — —

Something you fry food in.
Change the first letter.

3 — — — —

The past tense of *run*.
Take away the second vowel.

2 — — — —

You need an umbrella when this falls.
Take away the first letter.

1 — — — — —

b r a i n

Name _____

All wet

Read the clues, then write the words.
Start at the bottom and climb to the top.

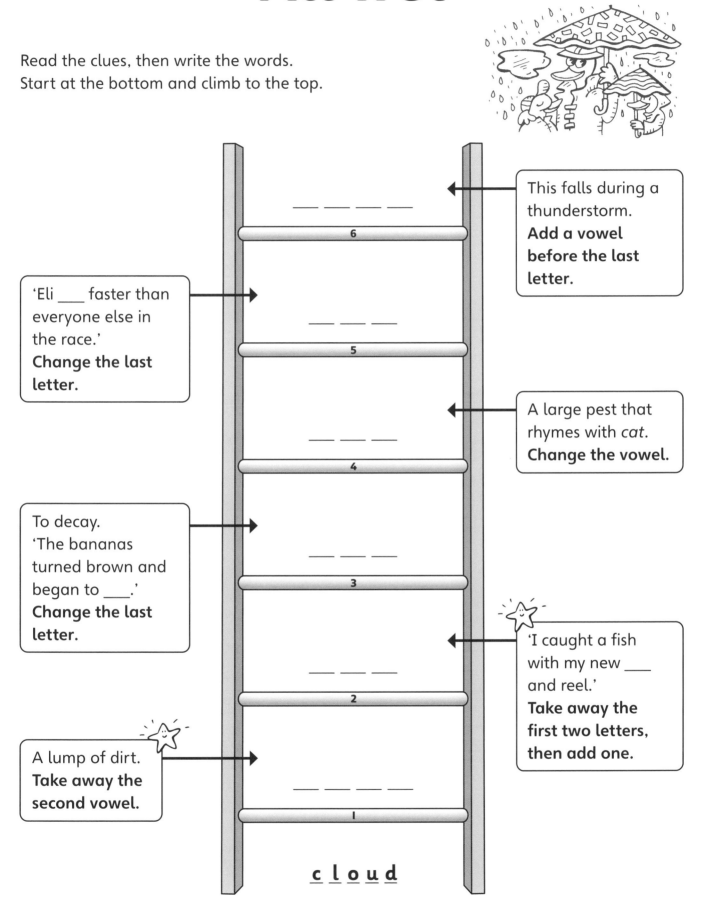

This falls during a thunderstorm.
Add a vowel before the last letter.

__ __ __ __   6

'Eli ___ faster than everyone else in the race.'
Change the last letter.

__ __ __   5

A large pest that rhymes with *cat*.
Change the vowel.

__ __ __   4

To decay. 'The bananas turned brown and began to ___.'
Change the last letter.

__ __ __   3

'I caught a fish with my new ___ and reel.'
Take away the first two letters, then add one.

__ __ __   2

A lump of dirt.
Take away the second vowel.

__ __ __ __   1

<u>c l o u d</u>

Take a seat

Read the clues, then write the words.
Start at the bottom and climb to the top.

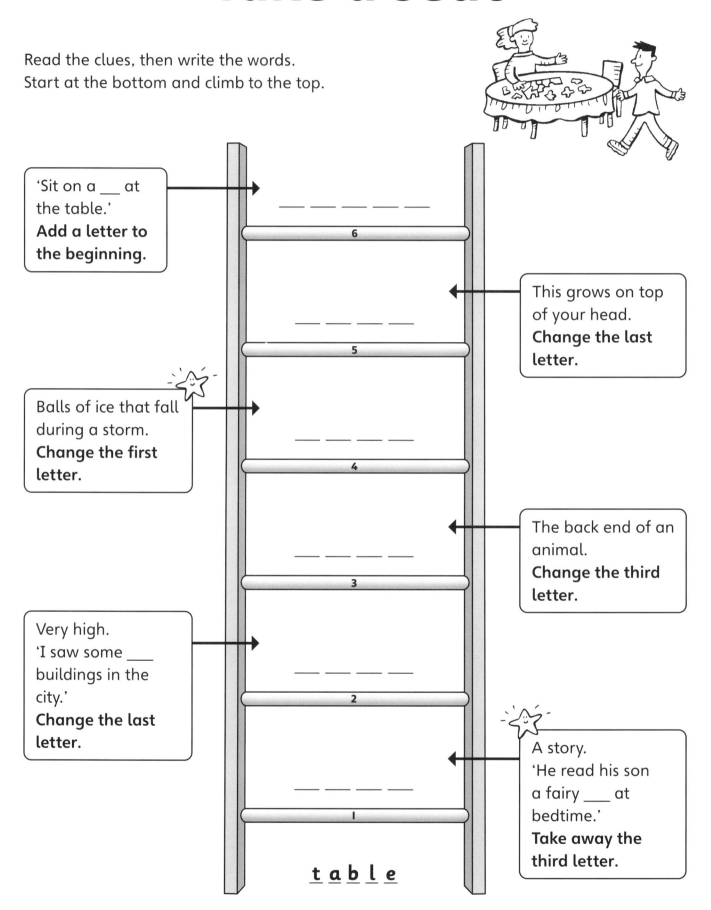

'Sit on a __ at the table.'
Add a letter to the beginning.

— — — — — —
6

This grows on top of your head.
Change the last letter.

— — — — —
5

Balls of ice that fall during a storm.
Change the first letter.

— — — —
4

The back end of an animal.
Change the third letter.

— — — —
3

Very high.
'I saw some ___ buildings in the city.'
Change the last letter.

— — — — —
2

A story.
'He read his son a fairy ___ at bedtime.'
Take away the third letter.

— — — —
1

<u>t</u> <u>a</u> <u>b</u> <u>l</u> <u>e</u>

Daily Word Ladders for Fluency **SCHOLASTIC**

Woodcutter

Read the clues, then write the words.
Start at the bottom and climb to the top.

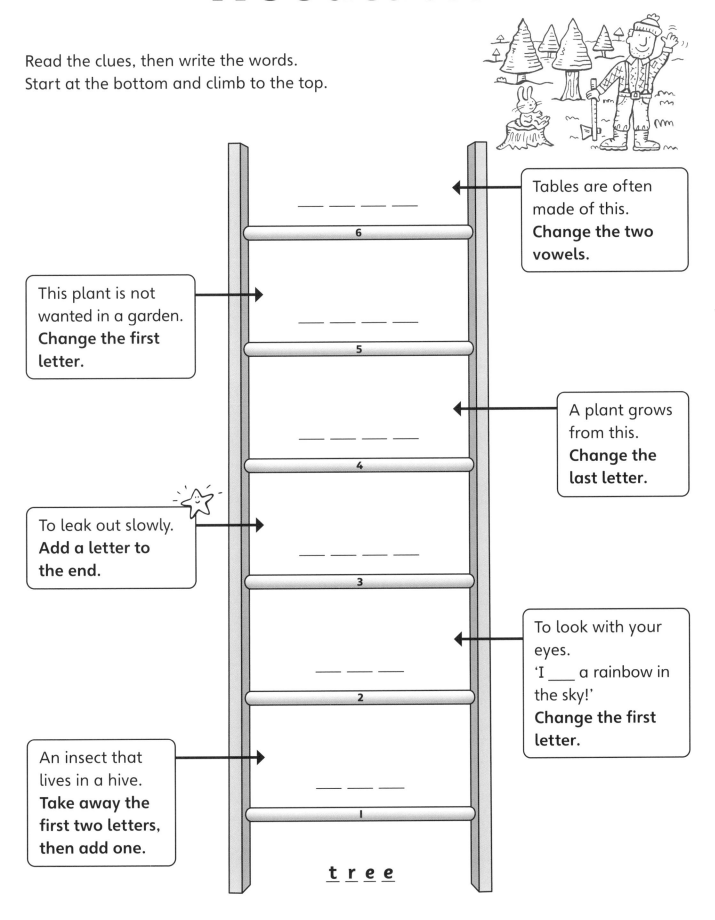

Tables are often made of this. **Change the two vowels.**

6 _ _ _ _

This plant is not wanted in a garden. **Change the first letter.**

5 _ _ _ _

A plant grows from this. **Change the last letter.**

4 _ _ _ _

To leak out slowly. **Add a letter to the end.**

3 _ _ _ _

To look with your eyes. 'I ___ a rainbow in the sky!' **Change the first letter.**

2 _ _ _

An insect that lives in a hive. **Take away the first two letters, then add one.**

1 _ _ _

<u>t r e e</u>

Daily journey

Read the clues, then write the words.
Start at the bottom and climb to the top.

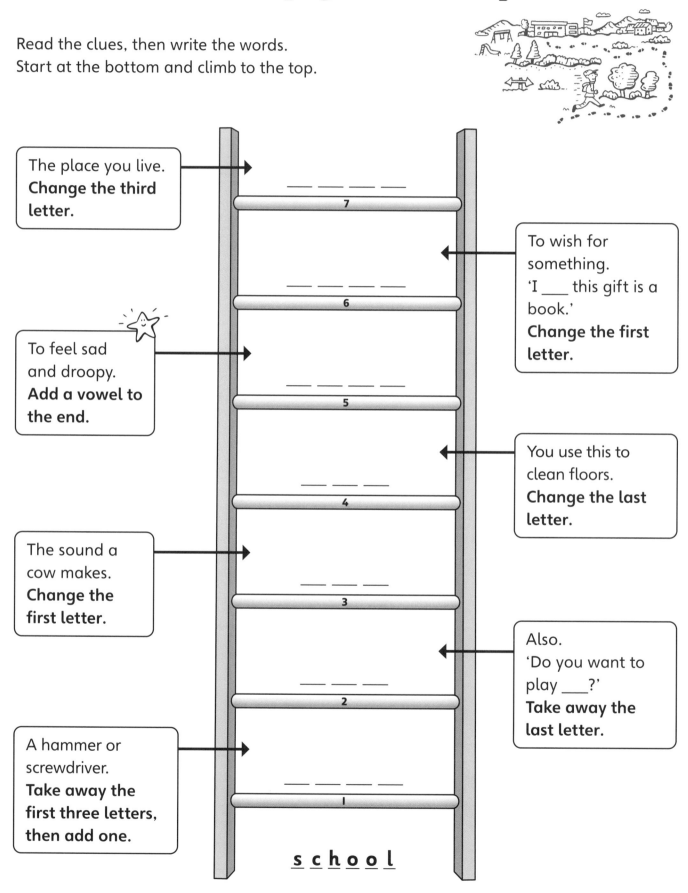

The place you live. **Change the third letter.**

7 _ _ _ _ _

To wish for something. 'I ___ this gift is a book.' **Change the first letter.**

6 _ _ _ _ _

To feel sad and droopy. **Add a vowel to the end.**

5 _ _ _ _ _

You use this to clean floors. **Change the last letter.**

4 _ _ _ _

The sound a cow makes. **Change the first letter.**

3 _ _ _ _

Also. 'Do you want to play ___?' **Take away the last letter.**

2 _ _ _ _

A hammer or screwdriver. **Take away the first three letters, then add one.**

1 _ _ _ _

s c h o o l

Daily Word Ladders for Fluency **SCHOLASTIC**

Name _____

Good books

Read the clues, then write the words.
Start at the bottom and climb to the top.

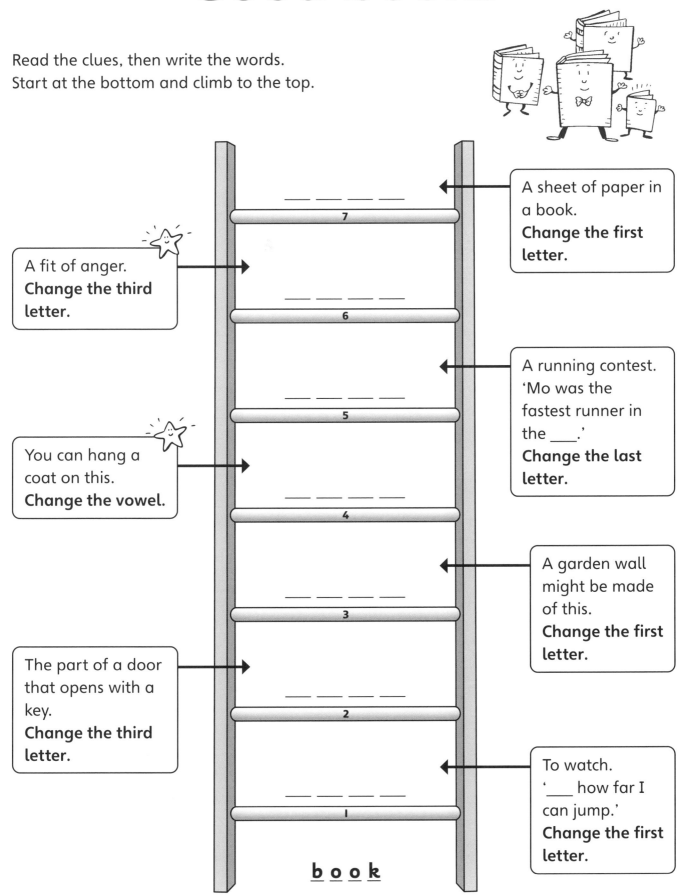

A sheet of paper in a book.
Change the first letter.

A fit of anger.
Change the third letter.

7 _ _ _ _ _

6 _ _ _ _

A running contest. 'Mo was the fastest runner in the ___.'
Change the last letter.

You can hang a coat on this.
Change the vowel.

5 _ _ _ _

4 _ _ _ _

A garden wall might be made of this.
Change the first letter.

The part of a door that opens with a key.
Change the third letter.

3 _ _ _ _

2 _ _ _ _

To watch. '___ how far I can jump.'
Change the first letter.

1 _ _ _ _

<u>b o o k</u>

Furry friends

Read the clues, then write the words.
Start at the bottom and climb to the top.

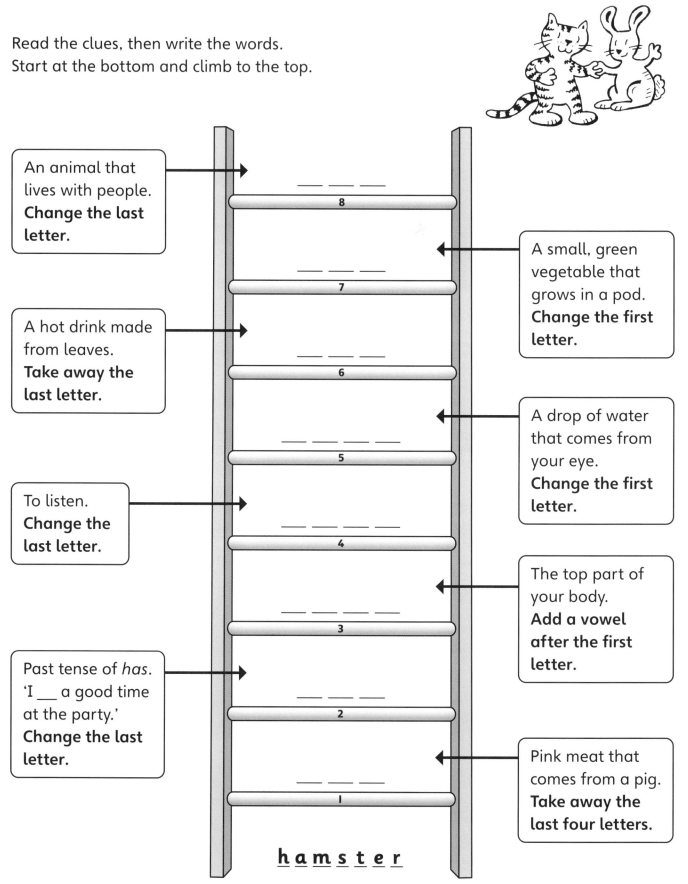

An animal that lives with people. **Change the last letter.**

A small, green vegetable that grows in a pod. **Change the first letter.**

A hot drink made from leaves. **Take away the last letter.**

A drop of water that comes from your eye. **Change the first letter.**

To listen. **Change the last letter.**

The top part of your body. **Add a vowel after the first letter.**

Past tense of *has*. 'I ___ a good time at the party.' **Change the last letter.**

Pink meat that comes from a pig. **Take away the last four letters.**

8

7

6

5

4

3

2

1

h a m s t e r

Name _____

Time flies

Read the clues, then write the words.
Start at the bottom and climb to the top.

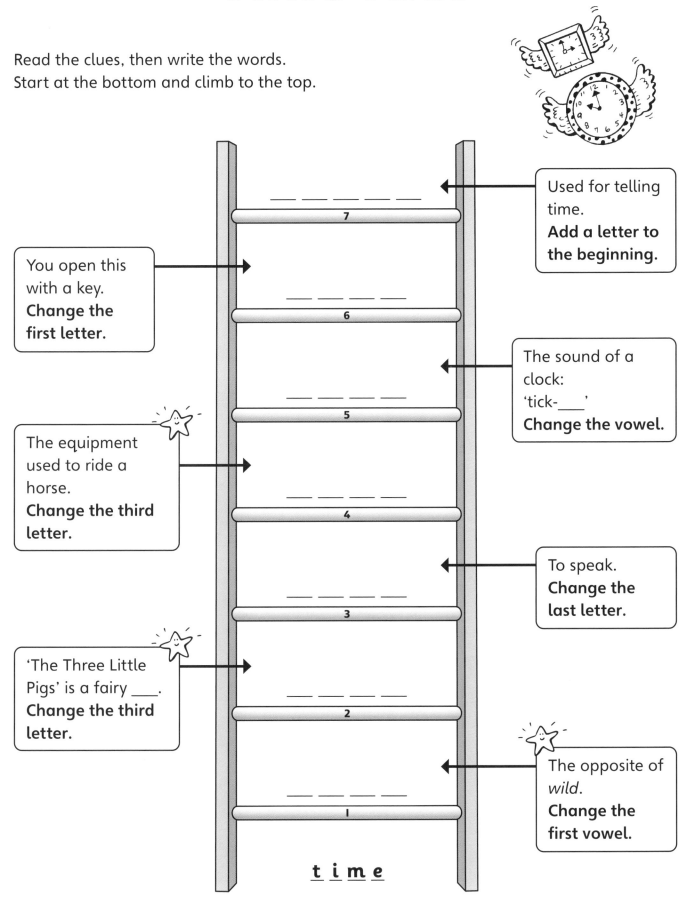

Used for telling time.
Add a letter to the beginning.

7 _ _ _ _ _ _

You open this with a key.
Change the first letter.

6 _ _ _ _ _

The sound of a clock: 'tick-___'
Change the vowel.

5 _ _ _ _ _

The equipment used to ride a horse.
Change the third letter.

4 _ _ _ _ _

To speak.
Change the last letter.

3 _ _ _ _ _

'The Three Little Pigs' is a fairy ___.
Change the third letter.

2 _ _ _ _ _

The opposite of *wild*.
Change the first vowel.

1 _ _ _ _ _

t i m e

Country living

Read the clues, then write the words.
Start at the bottom and climb to the top.

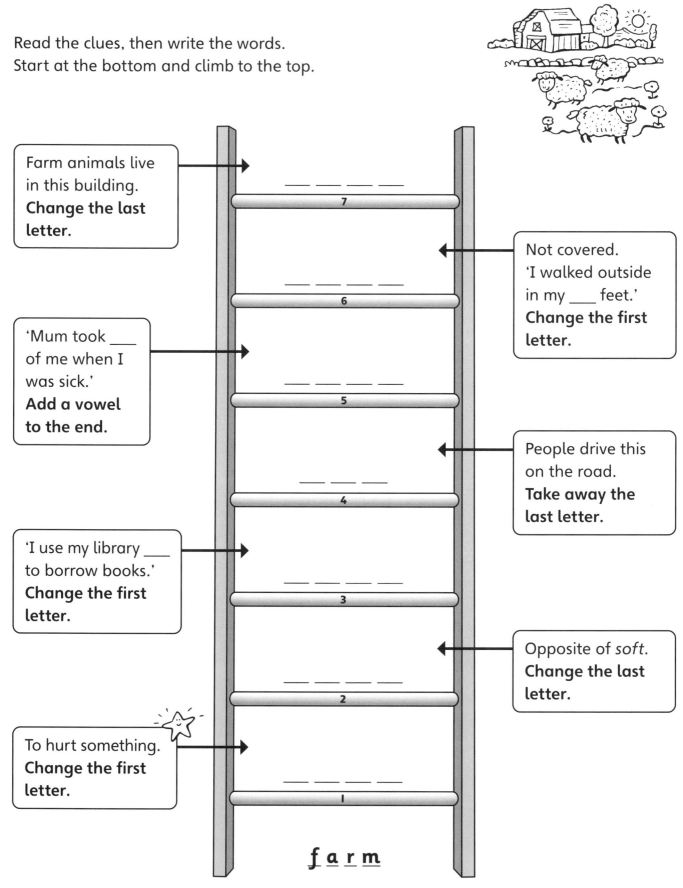

Farm animals live in this building. **Change the last letter.**
→ 7 _ _ _ _ _

Not covered. 'I walked outside in my ___ feet.' **Change the first letter.**
← 6 _ _ _ _ _

'Mum took ___ of me when I was sick.' **Add a vowel to the end.**
→ 5 _ _ _ _ _

People drive this on the road. **Take away the last letter.**
← 4 _ _ _ _

'I use my library ___ to borrow books.' **Change the first letter.**
→ 3 _ _ _ _

Opposite of *soft*. **Change the last letter.**
← 2 _ _ _ _

To hurt something. **Change the first letter.**
→ 1 _ _ _ _

f a r m

Name _____

Fun for everyone

Read the clues, then write the words.
Start at the bottom and climb to the top.

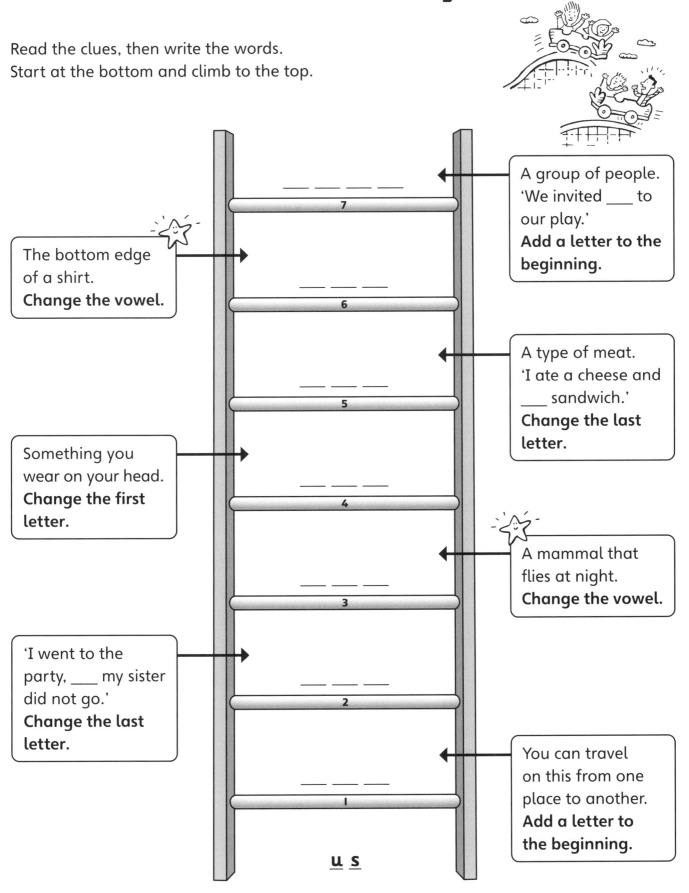

7 — — — — —

A group of people.
'We invited ___ to our play.'
Add a letter to the beginning.

The bottom edge of a shirt.
Change the vowel.

6 — — — —

5 — — — —

A type of meat.
'I ate a cheese and ___ sandwich.'
Change the last letter.

Something you wear on your head.
Change the first letter.

4 — — — —

3 — — — —

A mammal that flies at night.
Change the vowel.

'I went to the party, ___ my sister did not go.'
Change the last letter.

2 — — — —

1 — — —

You can travel on this from one place to another.
Add a letter to the beginning.

u s

Photocopiable

Name _____

Beautiful day

Read the clues, then write the words.
Start at the bottom and climb to the top.

The sun does this during the day. **Take away the first letter, then add two.**

7 ____ ____ ____ ____ ____ ____

Healthy or well. 'I didn't feel great last night but I'm ___ now.' **Change the third letter.**

6 ____ ____ ____ ____

This burns in a fireplace. **Change the first vowel.**

5 ____ ____ ____ ____

The money paid for a train ticket. **Add a letter to the end.**

4 ____ ____ ____ ____

A long way. 'He threw the ball ___ away.' **Change the vowel.**

3 ____ ____ ____

The hair on an animal. **Change the last letter.**

2 ____ ____ ____

'We always have ___ playing this game.' **Change the first letter.**

1 ____ ____ ____

<u>s</u> <u>u</u> <u>n</u>

Daily Word Ladders for Fluency **SCHOLASTIC**

Good scents

Read the clues, then write the words.
Start at the bottom and climb to the top.

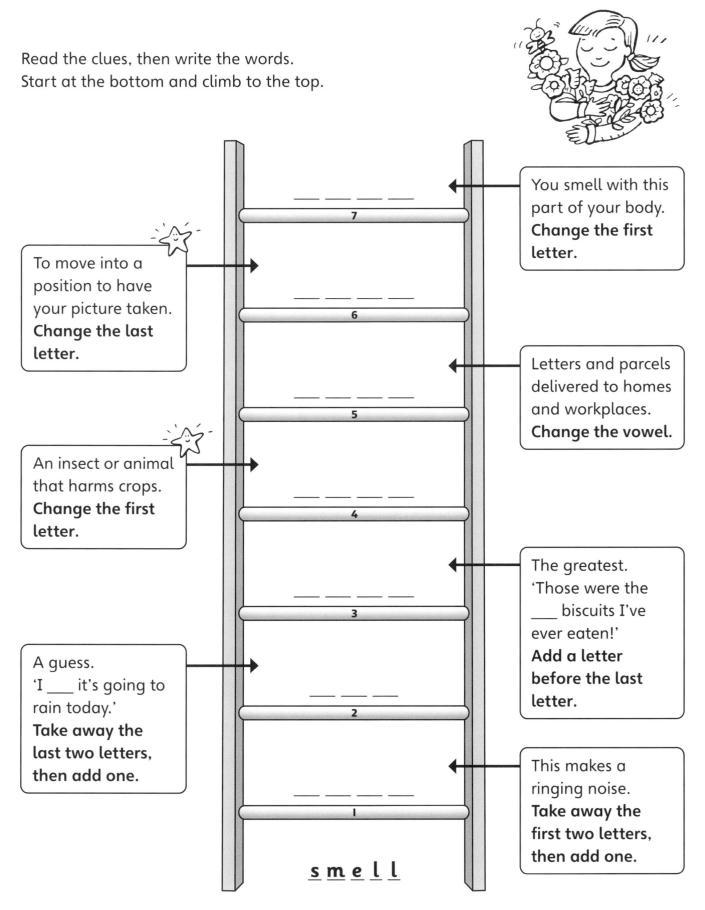

7 _ _ _ _ _

You smell with this part of your body. **Change the first letter.**

To move into a position to have your picture taken. **Change the last letter.**

6 _ _ _ _ _

5 _ _ _ _ _

Letters and parcels delivered to homes and workplaces. **Change the vowel.**

An insect or animal that harms crops. **Change the first letter.**

4 _ _ _ _ _

3 _ _ _ _ _

The greatest. 'Those were the ___ biscuits I've ever eaten!' **Add a letter before the last letter.**

A guess. 'I ___ it's going to rain today.' **Take away the last two letters, then add one.**

2 _ _ _ _

1 _ _ _ _ _

This makes a ringing noise. **Take away the first two letters, then add one.**

s m e l l

Meadow friends

Read the clues, then write the words.
Start at the bottom and climb to the top.

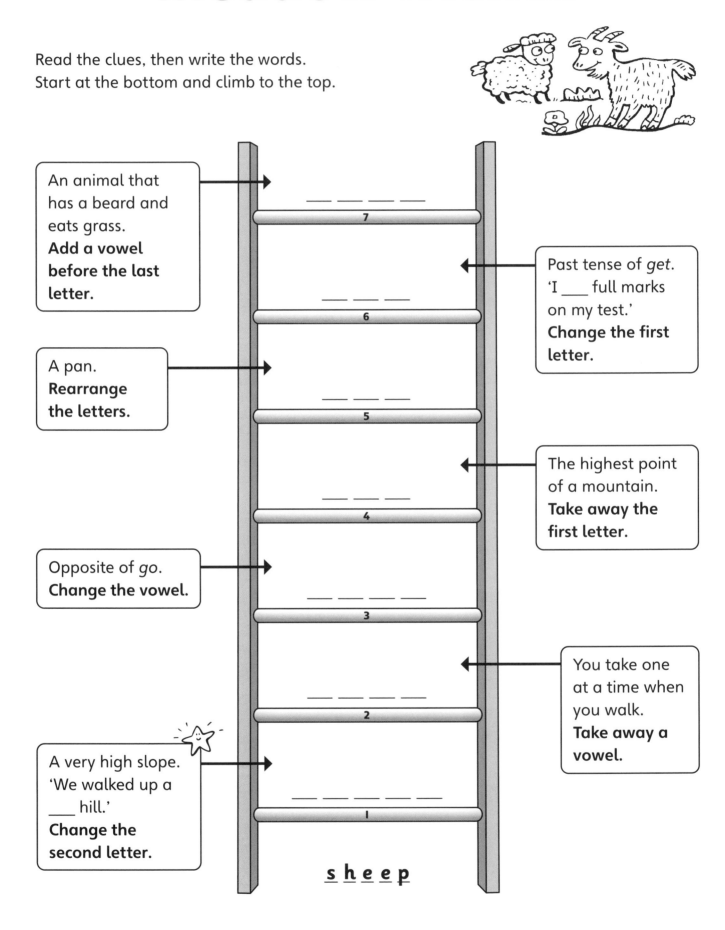

An animal that has a beard and eats grass. **Add a vowel before the last letter.**

7 _ _ _ _ _

Past tense of *get*. 'I ___ full marks on my test.' **Change the first letter.**

6 _ _ _ _

A pan. **Rearrange the letters.**

5 _ _ _

The highest point of a mountain. **Take away the first letter.**

4 _ _ _ _

Opposite of *go*. **Change the vowel.**

3 _ _ _ _ _

You take one at a time when you walk. **Take away a vowel.**

2 _ _ _ _ _

A very high slope. 'We walked up a ___ hill.' **Change the second letter.**

1 _ _ _ _ _

<u>s</u> <u>h</u> <u>e</u> <u>e</u> <u>p</u>

Name _____

Gentle breeze

Read the clues, then write the words.
Start at the bottom and climb to the top.

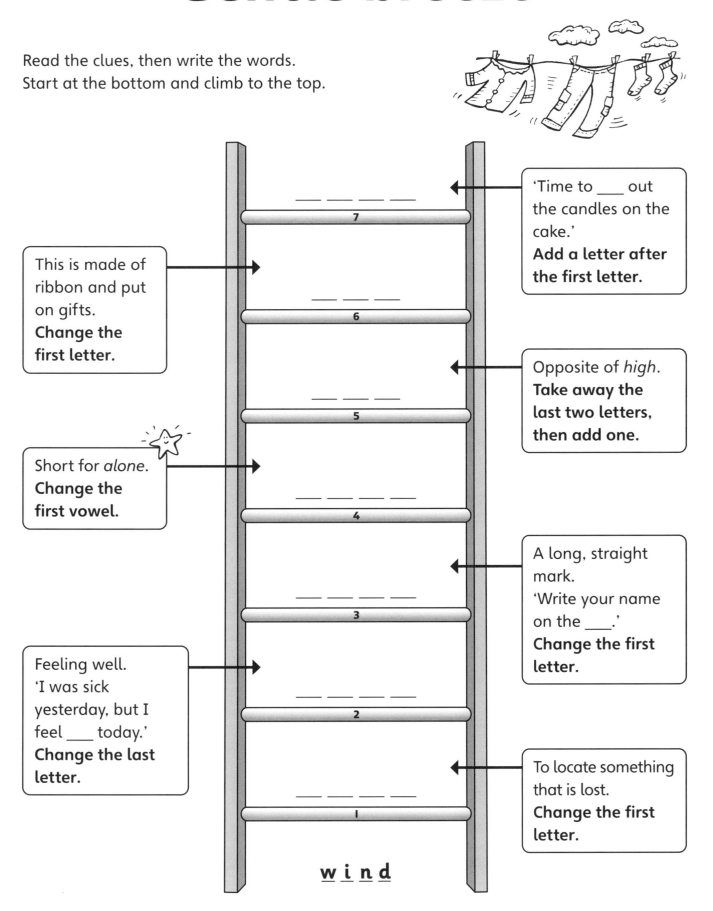

7 — — — — —

'Time to ___ out the candles on the cake.'
Add a letter after the first letter.

6 — — — —

This is made of ribbon and put on gifts.
Change the first letter.

5 — — — —

Opposite of *high*.
Take away the last two letters, then add one.

4 — — — — —

Short for *alone*.
Change the first vowel.

3 — — — — —

A long, straight mark.
'Write your name on the ___.'
Change the first letter.

2 — — — —

Feeling well.
'I was sick yesterday, but I feel ___ today.'
Change the last letter.

1 — — — —

To locate something that is lost.
Change the first letter.

<u>w</u> <u>i</u> <u>n</u> <u>d</u>

Name _____

Taking a dip

Read the clues, then write the words.
Start at the bottom and climb to the top.

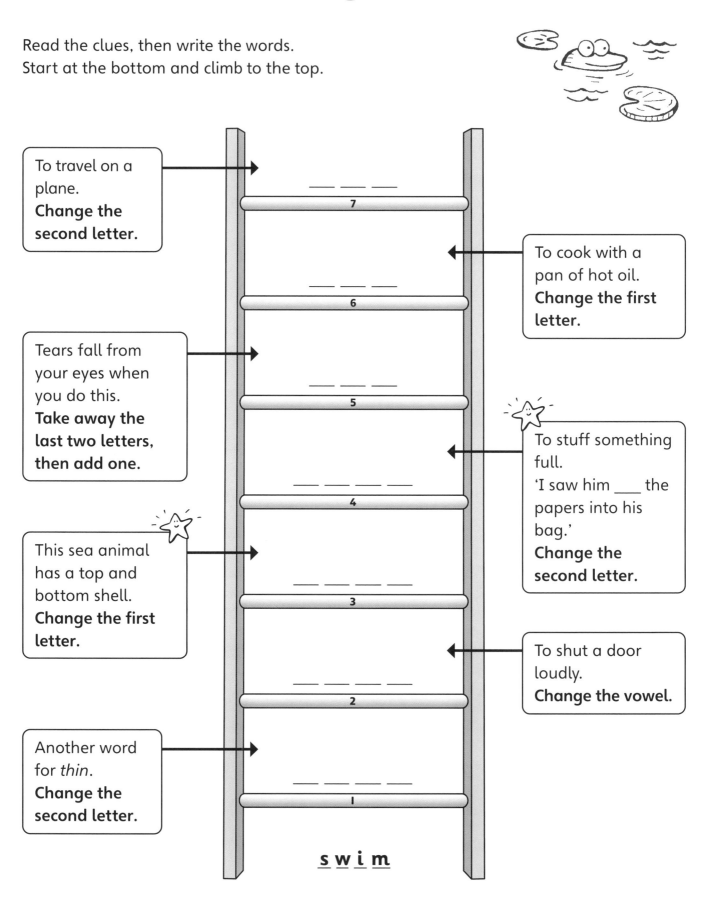

To travel on a plane.
Change the second letter.

→ 7 _ _ _ _

← To cook with a pan of hot oil. **Change the first letter.**

6 _ _ _ _

Tears fall from your eyes when you do this. **Take away the last two letters, then add one.**

→ 5 _ _ _ _

← To stuff something full. 'I saw him ___ the papers into his bag.' **Change the second letter.**

4 _ _ _ _ _

This sea animal has a top and bottom shell. **Change the first letter.**

→ 3 _ _ _ _ _

← To shut a door loudly. **Change the vowel.**

2 _ _ _ _ _

Another word for *thin*. **Change the second letter.**

→ 1 _ _ _ _

<u>s</u> <u>w</u> <u>i</u> <u>m</u>

Daily Word Ladders for Fluency **SCHOLASTIC**

Open wide

Read the clues, then write the words.
Start at the bottom and climb to the top.

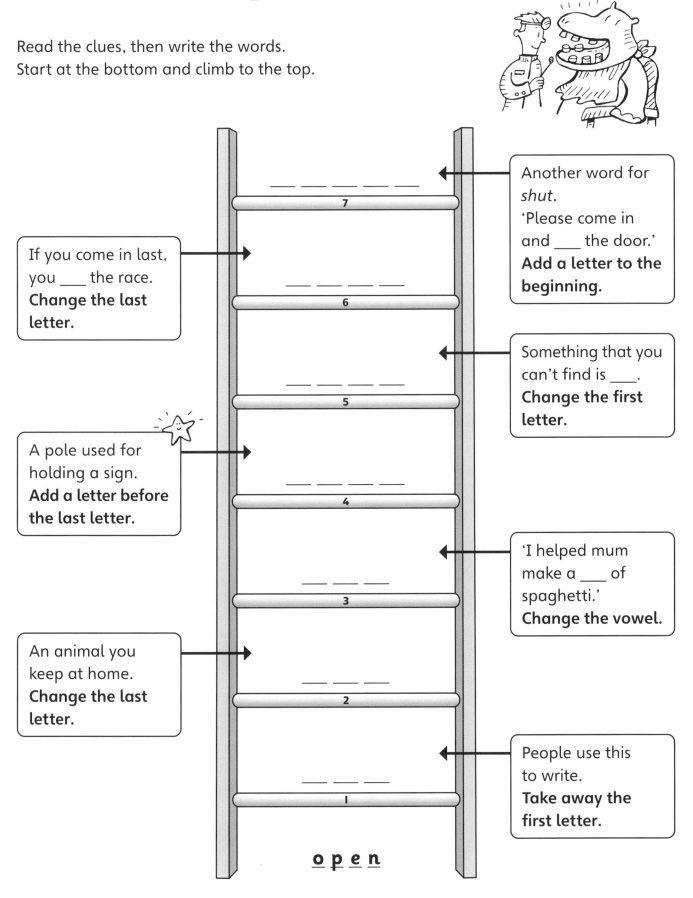

7 _ _ _ _ _ _

Another word for *shut*.
'Please come in and ___ the door.'
Add a letter to the beginning.

If you come in last, you ___ the race.
Change the last letter.

6 _ _ _ _ _

5 _ _ _ _ _

Something that you can't find is ___.
Change the first letter.

A pole used for holding a sign.
Add a letter before the last letter.

4 _ _ _ _ _

'I helped mum make a ___ of spaghetti.'
Change the vowel.

3 _ _ _ _

An animal you keep at home.
Change the last letter.

2 _ _ _ _

1 _ _ _

People use this to write.
Take away the first letter.

<u>o p e n</u>

Name _____

Feelings

Read the clues, then write the words.
Start at the bottom and climb to the top.

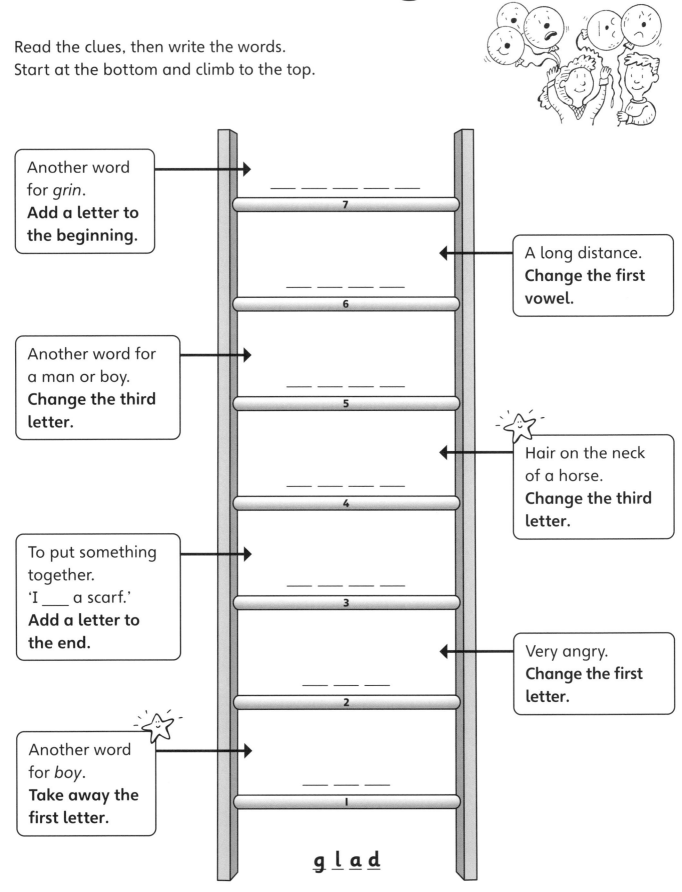

Another word for *grin*.
Add a letter to the beginning.

A long distance.
Change the first vowel.

Another word for a man or boy.
Change the third letter.

Hair on the neck of a horse.
Change the third letter.

To put something together.
'I ___ a scarf.'
Add a letter to the end.

Very angry.
Change the first letter.

Another word for *boy*.
Take away the first letter.

7

6

5

4

3

2

1

g l a d

Daily Word Ladders for Fluency **SCHOLASTIC**

Name _____

Fireworks

Read the clues, then write the words.
Start at the bottom and climb to the top.

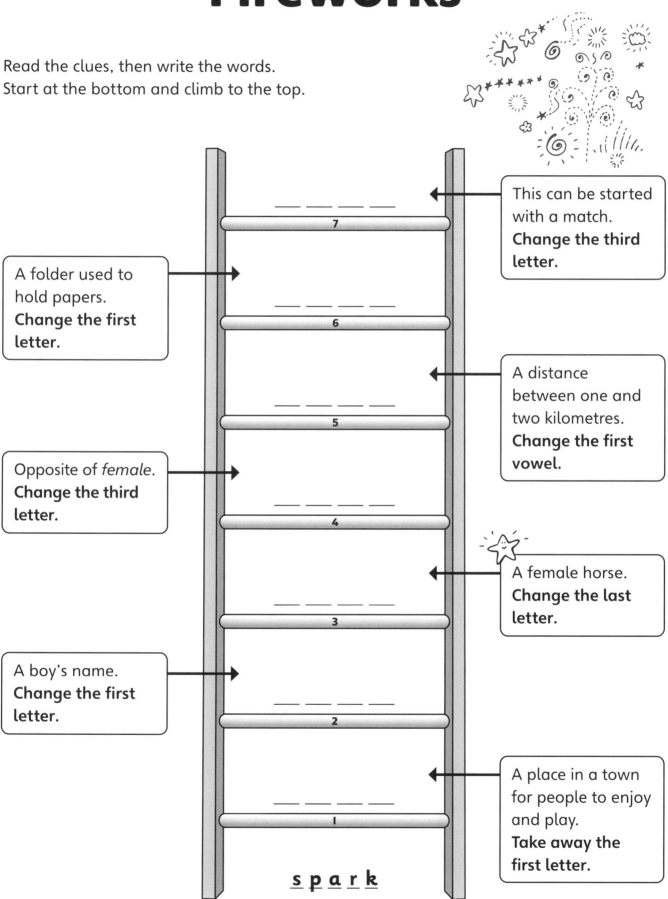

This can be started with a match. **Change the third letter.**

A folder used to hold papers. **Change the first letter.**

A distance between one and two kilometres. **Change the first vowel.**

Opposite of *female*. **Change the third letter.**

A female horse. **Change the last letter.**

A boy's name. **Change the first letter.**

A place in a town for people to enjoy and play. **Take away the first letter.**

7

6

5

4

3

2

1

s p a r k

On the move

Read the clues, then write the words.
Start at the bottom and climb to the top.

An automobile. **Change the last letter.**

Another word for *taxi*. **Change the first letter.**

You can do science experiments in this room. **Take away the third letter.**

A baby sheep. **Change the last letter.**

An animal that hurts its leg is ___. **Change the third letter.**

A large area of water 'We went boating on the ___.' **Change the first vowel.**

The same as. 'Your hat looks ___ my hat.' **Change the first letter.**

7 _ _ _ _

6 _ _ _ _

5 _ _ _

4 _ _ _ _

3 _ _ _

2 _ _ _ _

1 _ _ _ _

b i k e

Daily Word Ladders for Fluency **SCHOLASTIC**

Name _____

Car trouble

Read the clues, then write the words.
Start at the bottom and climb to the top.

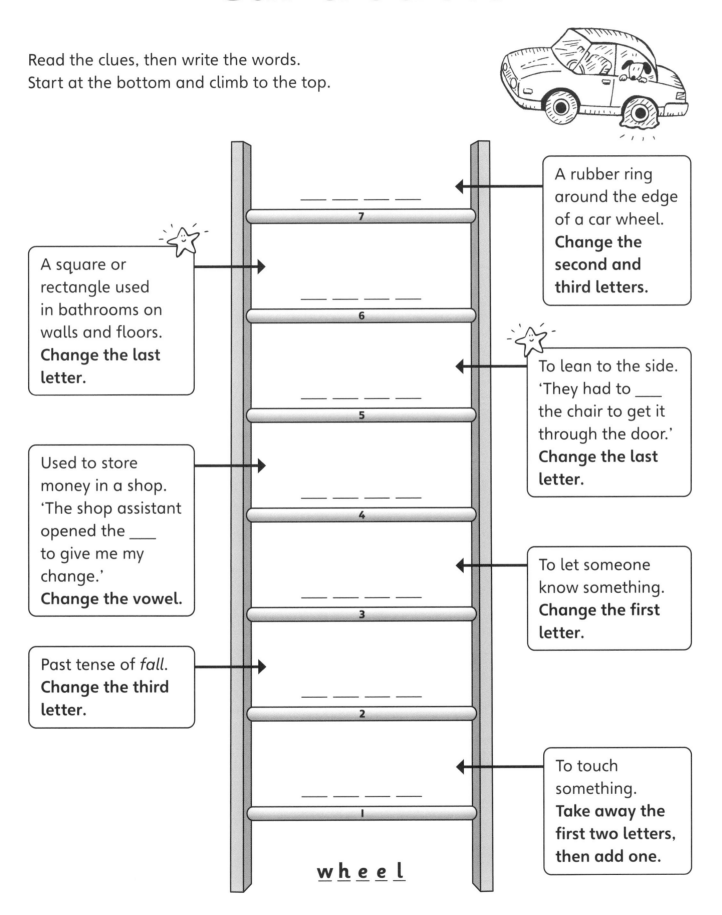

7 _ _ _ _ _

A rubber ring around the edge of a car wheel. **Change the second and third letters.**

6 _ _ _ _

A square or rectangle used in bathrooms on walls and floors. **Change the last letter.**

5 _ _ _ _

To lean to the side. 'They had to ___ the chair to get it through the door.' **Change the last letter.**

4 _ _ _ _

Used to store money in a shop. 'The shop assistant opened the ___ to give me my change.' **Change the vowel.**

3 _ _ _ _

To let someone know something. **Change the first letter.**

2 _ _ _ _

Past tense of *fall*. **Change the third letter.**

1 _ _ _ _

To touch something. **Take away the first two letters, then add one.**

w h e e l

Hair care

Read the clues, then write the words.
Start at the bottom and climb to the top.

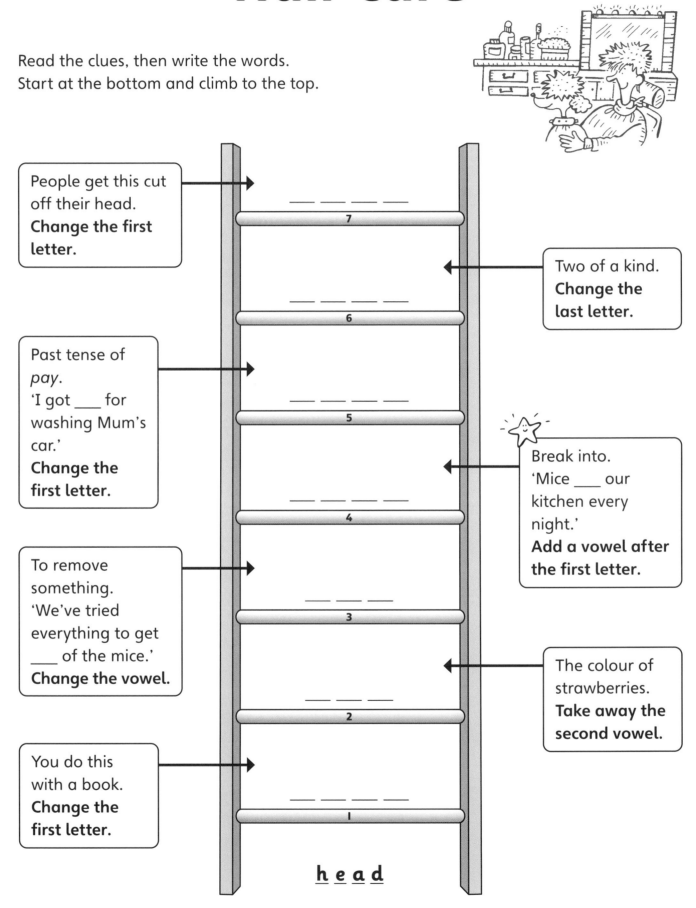

People get this cut off their head. **Change the first letter.**

— — — — —
7

Two of a kind. **Change the last letter.**

— — — — —
6

Past tense of *pay*. 'I got ___ for washing Mum's car.' **Change the first letter.**

— — — —
5

Break into. 'Mice ___ our kitchen every night.' **Add a vowel after the first letter.**

— — — —
4

To remove something. 'We've tried everything to get ___ of the mice.' **Change the vowel.**

— — —
3

The colour of strawberries. **Take away the second vowel.**

— — — —
2

You do this with a book. **Change the first letter.**

— — — —
1

<u>h e a d</u>

Daily Word Ladders for Fluency **SCHOLASTIC**

Hungry

Read the clues, then write the words.
Start at the bottom and climb to the top.

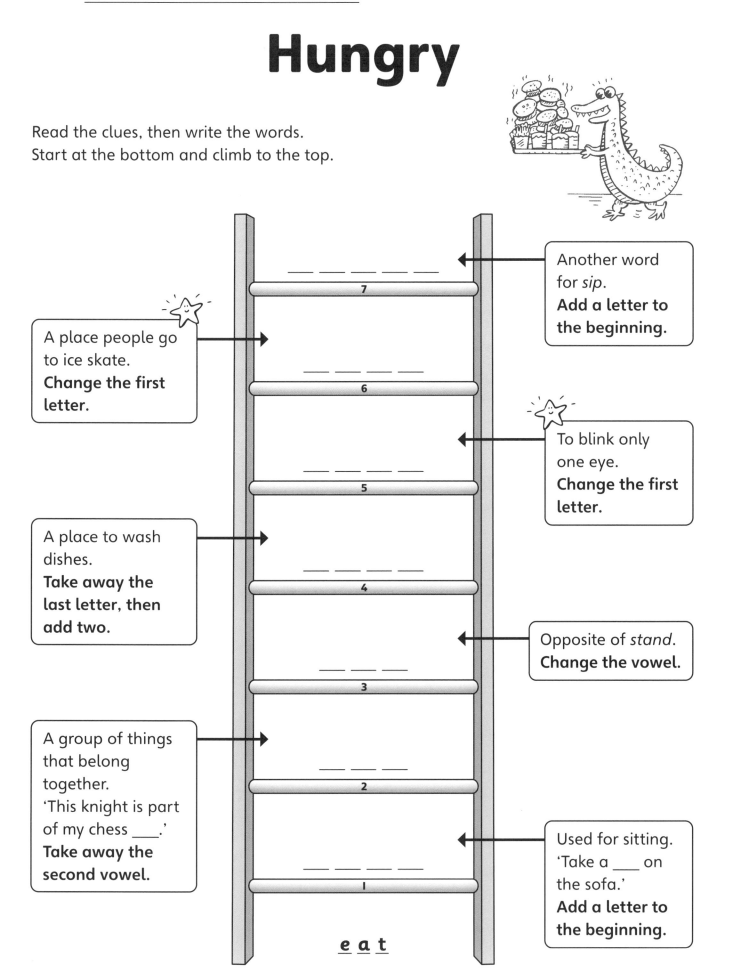

Another word for *sip*.
Add a letter to the beginning.

A place people go to ice skate.
Change the first letter.

To blink only one eye.
Change the first letter.

A place to wash dishes.
Take away the last letter, then add two.

Opposite of *stand*.
Change the vowel.

A group of things that belong together.
'This knight is part of my chess ___.'
Take away the second vowel.

Used for sitting.
'Take a ___ on the sofa.'
Add a letter to the beginning.

7

6

5

4

3

2

1

e a t

Name _____

Bookworm

Read the clues, then write the words.
Start at the bottom and climb to the top.

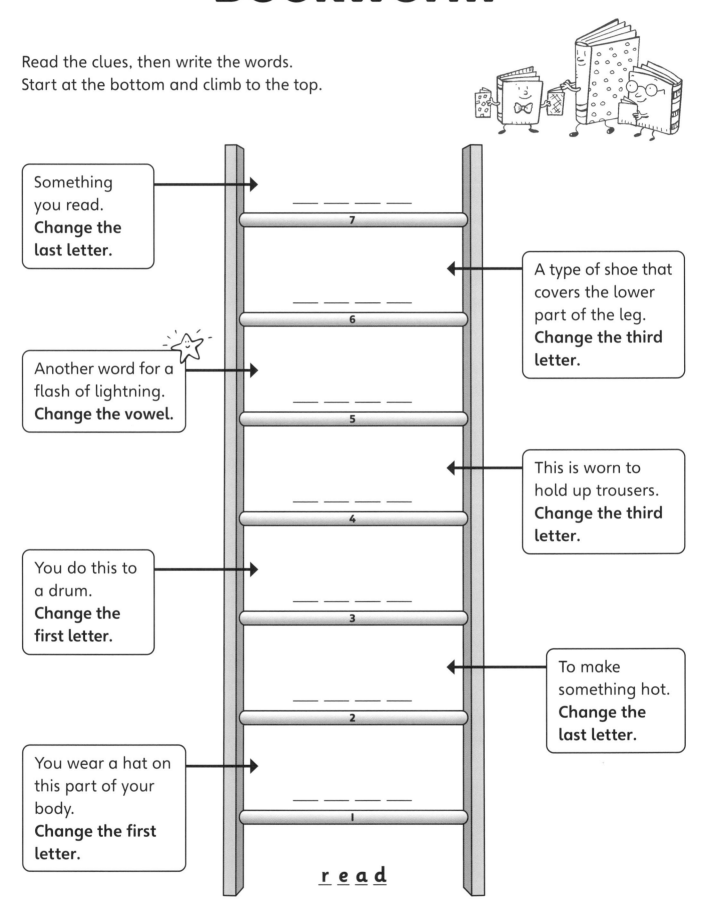

Something you read. **Change the last letter.**

7 _ _ _ _

A type of shoe that covers the lower part of the leg. **Change the third letter.**

6 _ _ _ _

Another word for a flash of lightning. **Change the vowel.**

5 _ _ _ _

This is worn to hold up trousers. **Change the third letter.**

4 _ _ _ _

You do this to a drum. **Change the first letter.**

3 _ _ _ _

To make something hot. **Change the last letter.**

2 _ _ _ _

You wear a hat on this part of your body. **Change the first letter.**

1 _ _ _ _

r e a d

Daily Word Ladders for Fluency **SCHOLASTIC**

Name _____

Peaks and valleys

Read the clues, then write the words.
Start at the bottom and climb to the top.

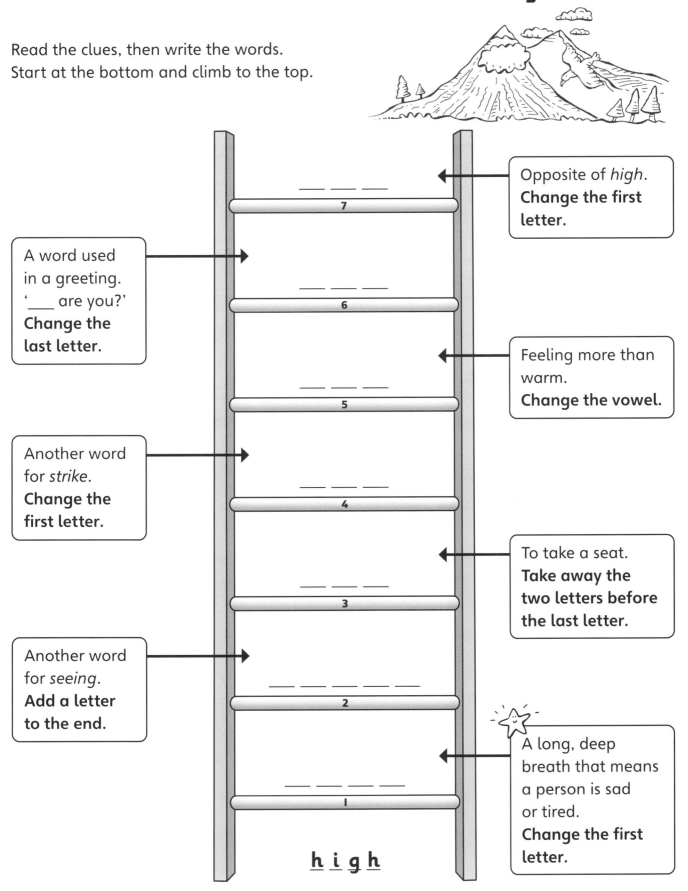

7 _ _ _ _

Opposite of *high*.
Change the first letter.

A word used
in a greeting.
'___ are you?'
**Change the
last letter.**

6 _ _ _ _

5 _ _ _ _

Feeling more than
warm.
Change the vowel.

Another word
for *strike*.
**Change the
first letter.**

4 _ _ _ _

To take a seat.
**Take away the
two letters before
the last letter.**

3 _ _ _ _

Another word
for *seeing*.
**Add a letter
to the end.**

2 _ _ _ _ _

A long, deep
breath that means
a person is sad
or tired.
**Change the first
letter.**

1 _ _ _ _ _

<u>h i g h</u>

Name _____

Go, go, go

Read the clues, then write the words.
Start at the bottom and climb to the top.

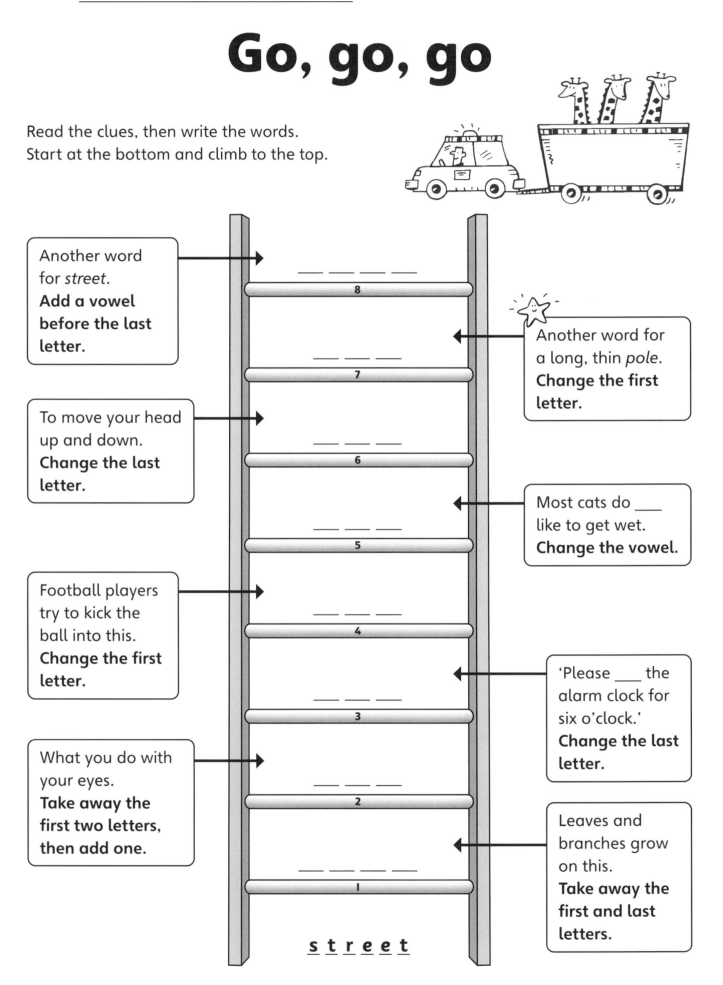

Another word for *street*. **Add a vowel before the last letter.**

→ _ _ _ _ _

8

Another word for a long, thin *pole*. **Change the first letter.**

_ _ _ _

7

To move your head up and down. **Change the last letter.**

→ _ _ _ _

6

Most cats do ___ like to get wet. **Change the vowel.**

_ _ _

5

Football players try to kick the ball into this. **Change the first letter.**

→ _ _ _

4

'Please ___ the alarm clock for six o'clock.' **Change the last letter.**

_ _ _

3

What you do with your eyes. **Take away the first two letters, then add one.**

→ _ _ _ _

2

Leaves and branches grow on this. **Take away the first and last letters.**

_ _ _ _ _

1

s t r e e t

Daily Word Ladders for Fluency ■SCHOLASTIC

Wild noises

Read the clues, then write the words.
Start at the bottom and climb to the top.

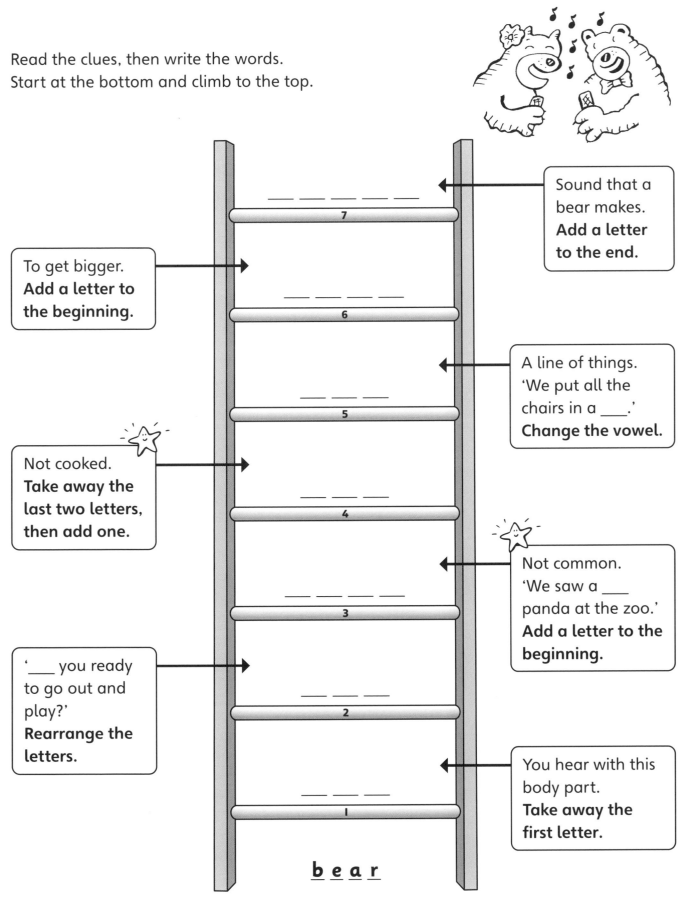

7 _ _ _ _ _ _

Sound that a bear makes. Add a letter to the end.

To get bigger. Add a letter to the beginning.

6 _ _ _ _

A line of things. 'We put all the chairs in a ___.' Change the vowel.

5 _ _ _ _

Not cooked. Take away the last two letters, then add one.

4 _ _ _

Not common. 'We saw a ___ panda at the zoo.' Add a letter to the beginning.

3 _ _ _ _ _

'___ you ready to go out and play?' Rearrange the letters.

2 _ _ _ _

You hear with this body part. Take away the first letter.

1 _ _ _ _

b e a r

Name _____

Life saver

Read the clues, then write the words.
Start at the bottom and climb to the top.

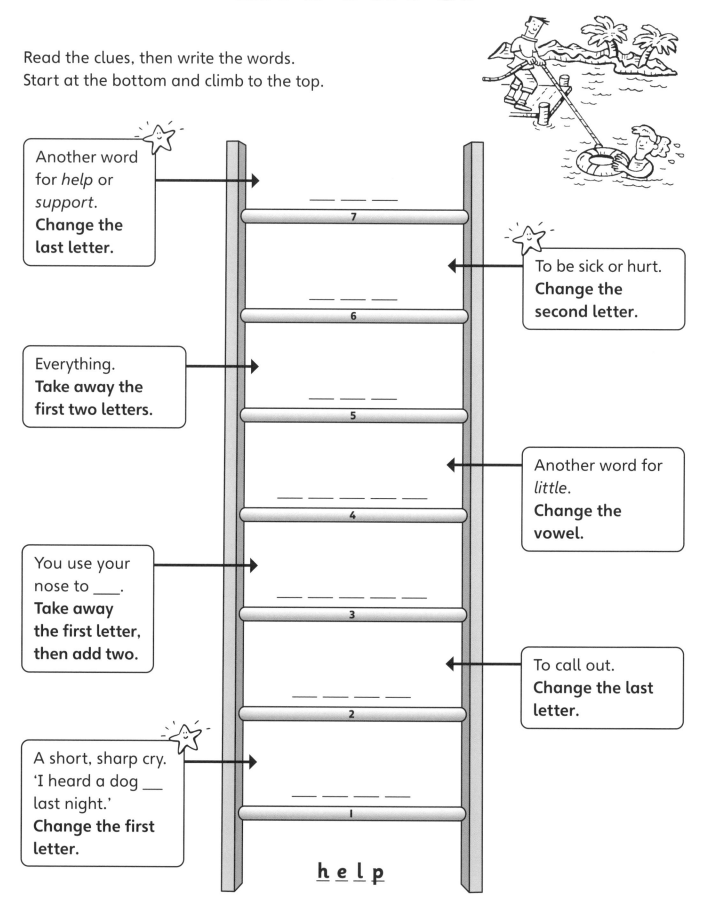

Another word for *help* or *support*.
Change the last letter.

To be sick or hurt.
Change the second letter.

Everything.
Take away the first two letters.

Another word for *little*.
Change the vowel.

You use your nose to ___.
Take away the first letter, then add two.

To call out.
Change the last letter.

A short, sharp cry. 'I heard a dog ___ last night.'
Change the first letter.

7

6

5

4

3

2

1

<u>h</u> <u>e</u> <u>l</u> <u>p</u>

Daily Word Ladders for Fluency **SCHOLASTIC**

Name _____

Bread and butter

Read the clues, then write the words.
Start at the bottom and climb to the top.

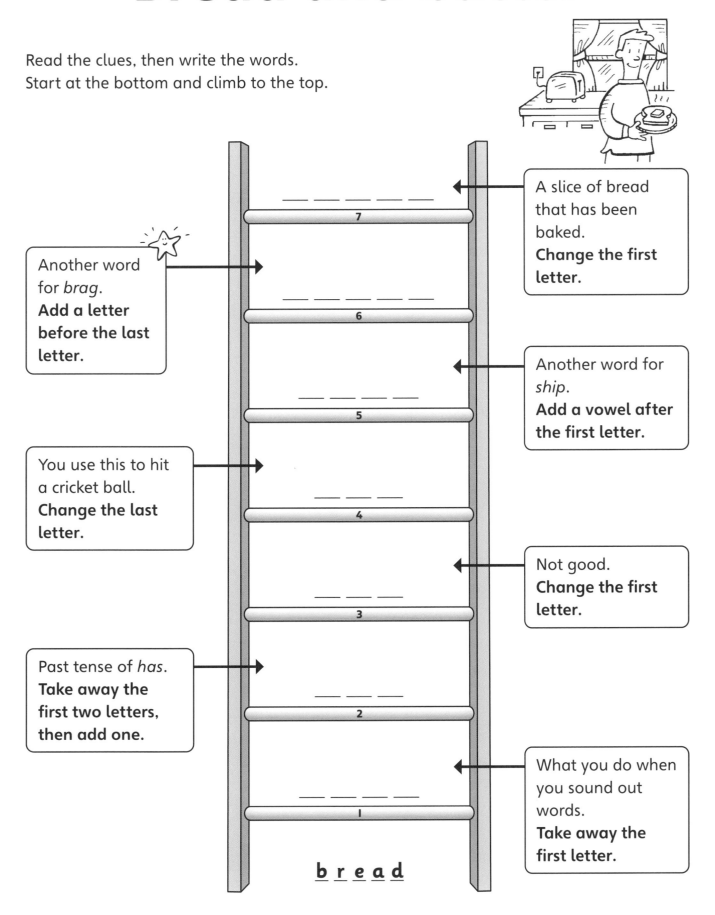

7 — A slice of bread that has been baked. **Change the first letter.**

Another word for *brag*. **Add a letter before the last letter.** → **6**

5 — Another word for *ship*. **Add a vowel after the first letter.**

You use this to hit a cricket ball. **Change the last letter.** → **4**

3 — Not good. **Change the first letter.**

Past tense of *has*. **Take away the first two letters, then add one.** → **2**

1 — What you do when you sound out words. **Take away the first letter.**

b r e a d

In the sky

Read the clues, then write the words.
Start at the bottom and climb to the top.

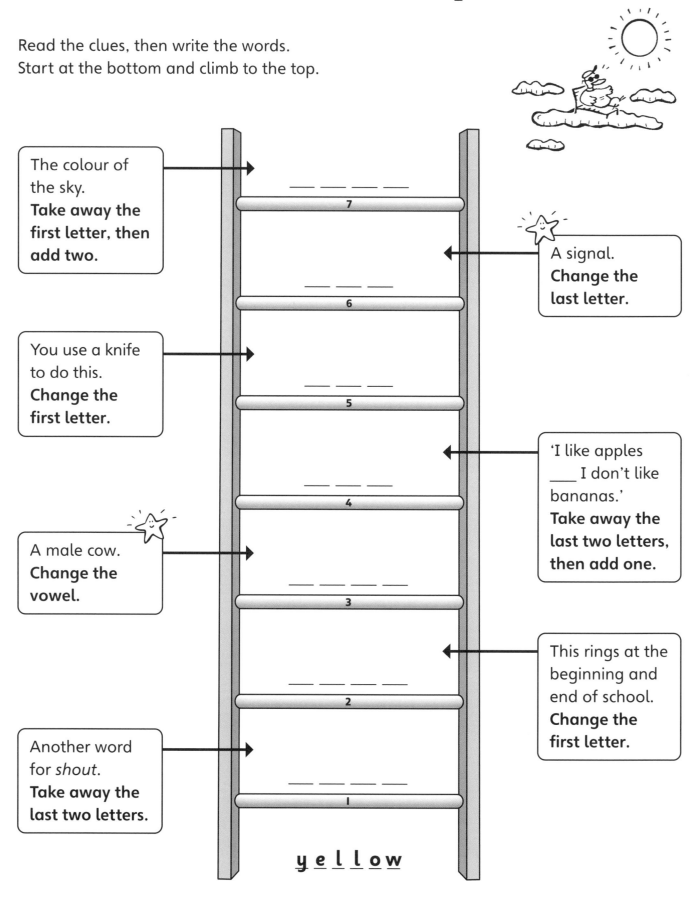

The colour of the sky. **Take away the first letter, then add two.**

A signal. **Change the last letter.**

You use a knife to do this. **Change the first letter.**

'I like apples ___ I don't like bananas.' **Take away the last two letters, then add one.**

A male cow. **Change the vowel.**

This rings at the beginning and end of school. **Change the first letter.**

Another word for *shout*. **Take away the last two letters.**

7
6
5
4
3
2
1

y e l l o w

Daily Word Ladders for Fluency **SCHOLASTIC**

Sailing

Read the clues, then write the words.
Start at the bottom and climb to the top.

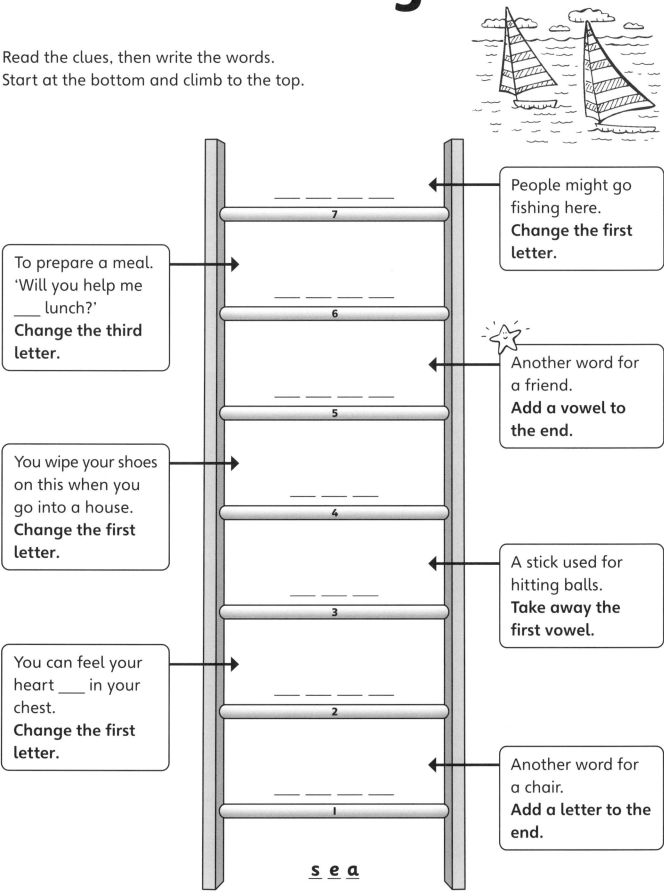

People might go fishing here. **Change the first letter.**

To prepare a meal. 'Will you help me ___ lunch?' **Change the third letter.**

Another word for a friend. **Add a vowel to the end.**

You wipe your shoes on this when you go into a house. **Change the first letter.**

A stick used for hitting balls. **Take away the first vowel.**

You can feel your heart ___ in your chest. **Change the first letter.**

Another word for a chair. **Add a letter to the end.**

s e a

Name _____

School days

Read the clues, then write the words.
Start at the bottom and climb to the top.

To put words on paper.
Change the second letter.

→ _ _ _ _ _ 7

6 _ _ _ _ _ ←

Opposite of *black*.
Change the vowel, then add a vowel to the end.

A word used to ask a question. '___ time is it?'
Take away the first vowel.

→ _ _ _ _ 5

4 _ _ _ _ _ ←

A grain used to make bread and cereal.
Take away the first letter, then add two.

Food that comes from animals.
Change the last letter.

→ _ _ _ _ 3

2 _ _ _ _ ←

Breakfast, lunch or dinner.
Change the first letter.

Something you can see and touch is this.
Change the last letter.

→ _ _ _ _ 1

r e a d

Daily Word Ladders for Fluency **SCHOLASTIC**

Toe-tapping tunes

Read the clues, then write the words.
Start at the bottom and climb to the top.

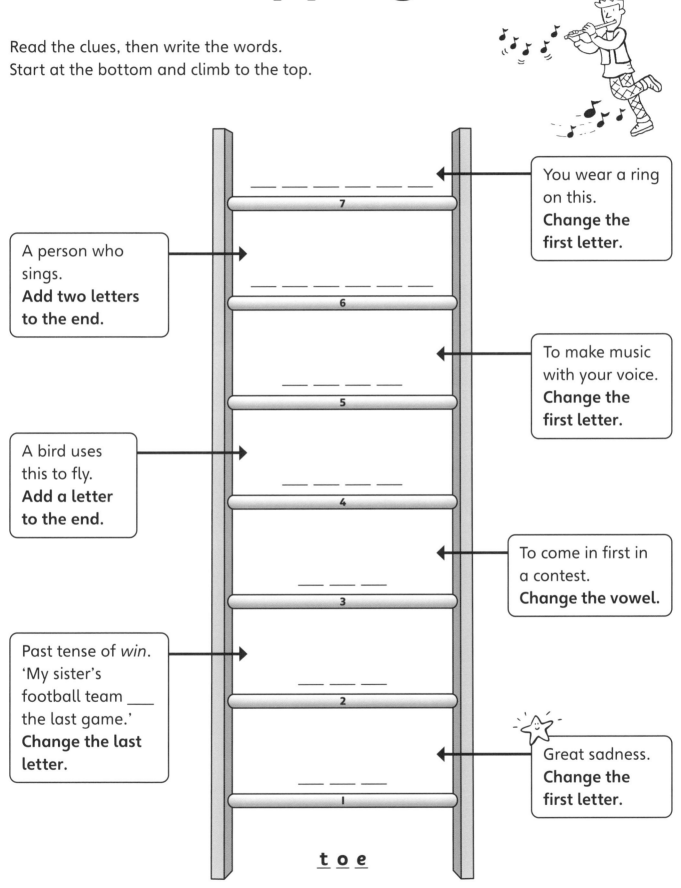

7 — — — — — —
You wear a ring on this. **Change the first letter.**

A person who sings. **Add two letters to the end.**
6 — — — — —

5 — — — —
To make music with your voice. **Change the first letter.**

A bird uses this to fly. **Add a letter to the end.**
4 — — — —

3 — — —
To come in first in a contest. **Change the vowel.**

Past tense of *win*. 'My sister's football team ___ the last game.' **Change the last letter.**
2 — — —

1 — — —
Great sadness. **Change the first letter.**

t o e

Name _____

Wonderful words

Read the clues, then write the words.
Start at the bottom and climb to the top.

YOU ARE
MY PAL

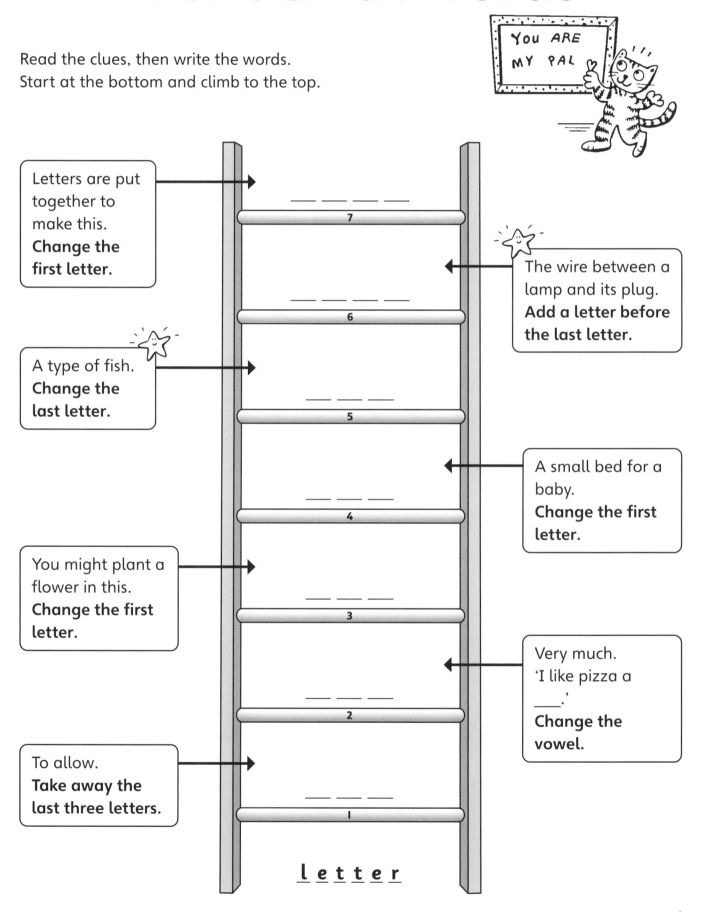

Letters are put together to make this. **Change the first letter.**

7 _ _ _ _ _

The wire between a lamp and its plug. **Add a letter before the last letter.**

6 _ _ _ _ _

A type of fish. **Change the last letter.**

5 _ _ _ _

A small bed for a baby. **Change the first letter.**

4 _ _ _

You might plant a flower in this. **Change the first letter.**

3 _ _ _

Very much. 'I like pizza a ___.' **Change the vowel.**

2 _ _ _

To allow. **Take away the last three letters.**

1 _ _ _

l e t t e r

Daily Word Ladders for Fluency **SCHOLASTIC**

Name _____

On your feet

Read the clues, then write the words.
Start at the bottom and climb to the top.

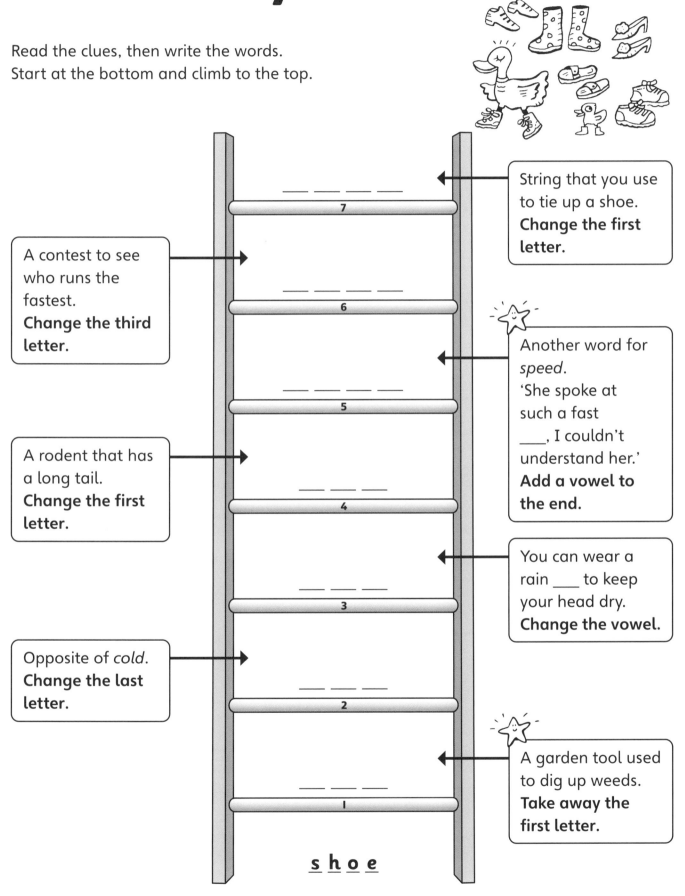

String that you use to tie up a shoe. **Change the first letter.**

A contest to see who runs the fastest. **Change the third letter.**

Another word for *speed*. 'She spoke at such a fast ___, I couldn't understand her.' **Add a vowel to the end.**

A rodent that has a long tail. **Change the first letter.**

You can wear a rain ___ to keep your head dry. **Change the vowel.**

Opposite of *cold*. **Change the last letter.**

A garden tool used to dig up weeds. **Take away the first letter.**

_s_ _h_ _o_ _e_

Name _____

Time's up

Read the clues, then write the words.
Start at the bottom and climb to the top.

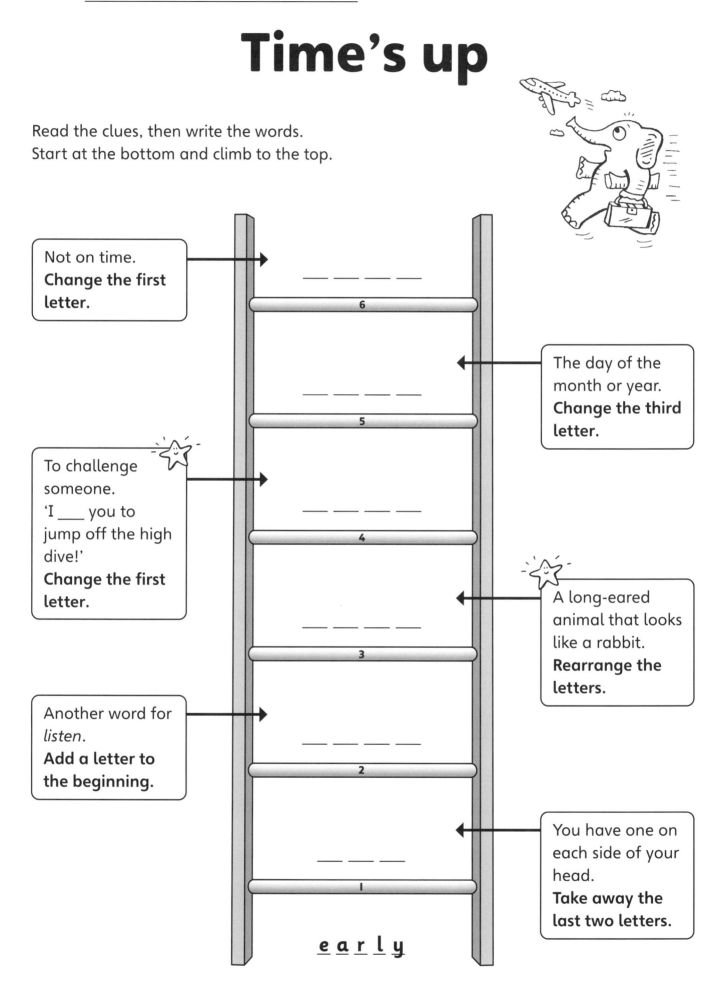

Not on time.
Change the first letter.

— — — — —
6

The day of the month or year. **Change the third letter.**

— — — — —
5

To challenge someone.
'I ___ you to jump off the high dive!'
Change the first letter.

— — — —
4

A long-eared animal that looks like a rabbit. **Rearrange the letters.**

— — — — —
3

Another word for *listen*.
Add a letter to the beginning.

— — — — —
2

You have one on each side of your head.
Take away the last two letters.

— — — —
1

<u>e a r l y</u>

Name _____

Directions

Read the clues, then write the words.
Start at the bottom and climb to the top.

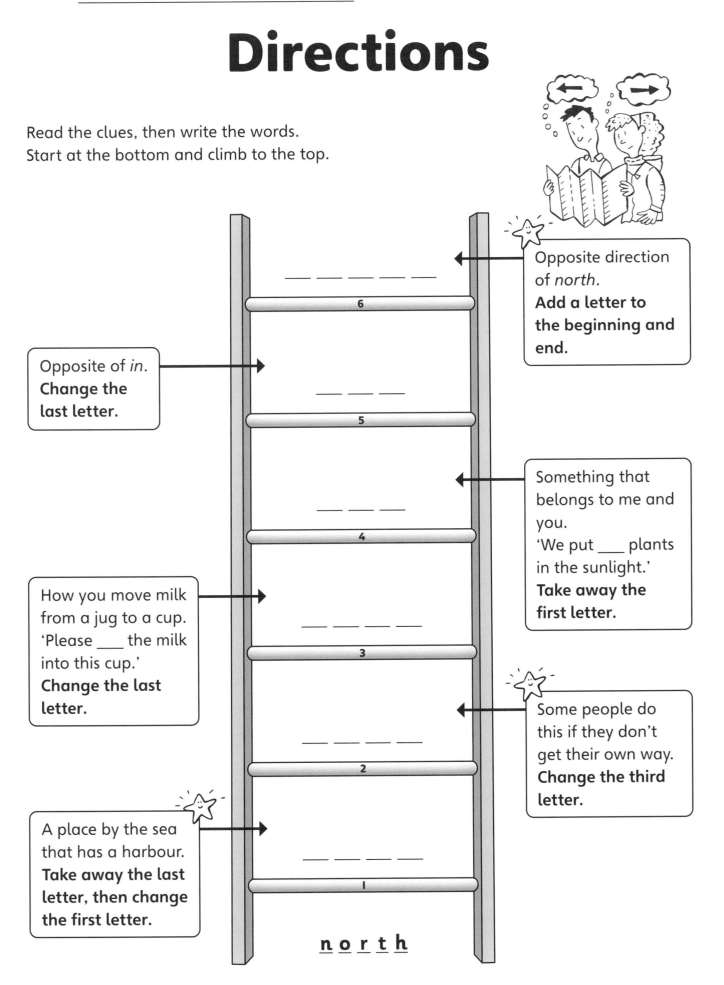

Opposite direction of *north*.
Add a letter to the beginning and end.

6 _ _ _ _ _ _

Opposite of *in*.
Change the last letter.

5 _ _ _ _

Something that belongs to me and you.
'We put ___ plants in the sunlight.'
Take away the first letter.

4 _ _ _ _

How you move milk from a jug to a cup.
'Please ___ the milk into this cup.'
Change the last letter.

3 _ _ _ _ _

Some people do this if they don't get their own way.
Change the third letter.

2 _ _ _ _ _

A place by the sea that has a harbour.
Take away the last letter, then change the first letter.

1 _ _ _ _

<u>n</u> <u>o</u> <u>r</u> <u>t</u> <u>h</u>

In the tree

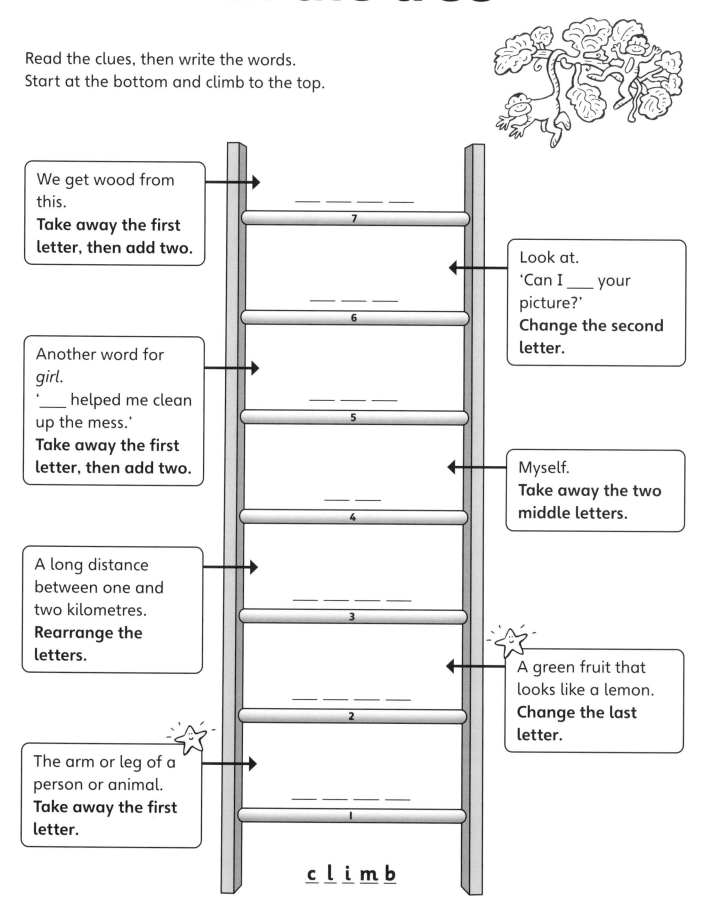

Read the clues, then write the words.
Start at the bottom and climb to the top.

We get wood from this.
Take away the first letter, then add two.

7 — — — — —

Look at.
'Can I ___ your picture?'
Change the second letter.

6 — — — —

Another word for *girl*.
'___ helped me clean up the mess.'
Take away the first letter, then add two.

5 — — — —

Myself.
Take away the two middle letters.

4 — —

A long distance between one and two kilometres.
Rearrange the letters.

3 — — — —

A green fruit that looks like a lemon.
Change the last letter.

2 — — — — —

The arm or leg of a person or animal.
Take away the first letter.

1 — — — —

<u>c</u> <u>l</u> <u>i</u> <u>m</u> <u>b</u>

Daily Word Ladders for Fluency **⚫SCHOLASTIC**

Brrrrr!

Name _____

Read the clues, then write the words.
Start at the bottom and climb to the top.

7 — __ __ __ __
Another word for *chilly*. **Change the first letter.**

6 — __ __ __ __
Past tense of *sell*. 'He ___ the car last night.' **Add a letter before the last letter.**

5 — __ __ __
A piece of ground with grass growing on it. **Change the last letter.**

4 — __ __ __
What a boy is to his parents. **Take away a vowel.**

3 — __ __ __ __
In a short time. 'I will be back ___.' **Take away the second letter.**

2 — __ __ __ __ __
You eat soup with this. **Change the last letter.**

1 — __ __ __ __ __
Thread is wrapped around this. **Take away the first letter, then add two.**

<u>c</u> <u>o</u> <u>o</u> <u>l</u>

Name _____

A clear view

Read the clues, then write the words.
Start at the bottom and climb to the top.

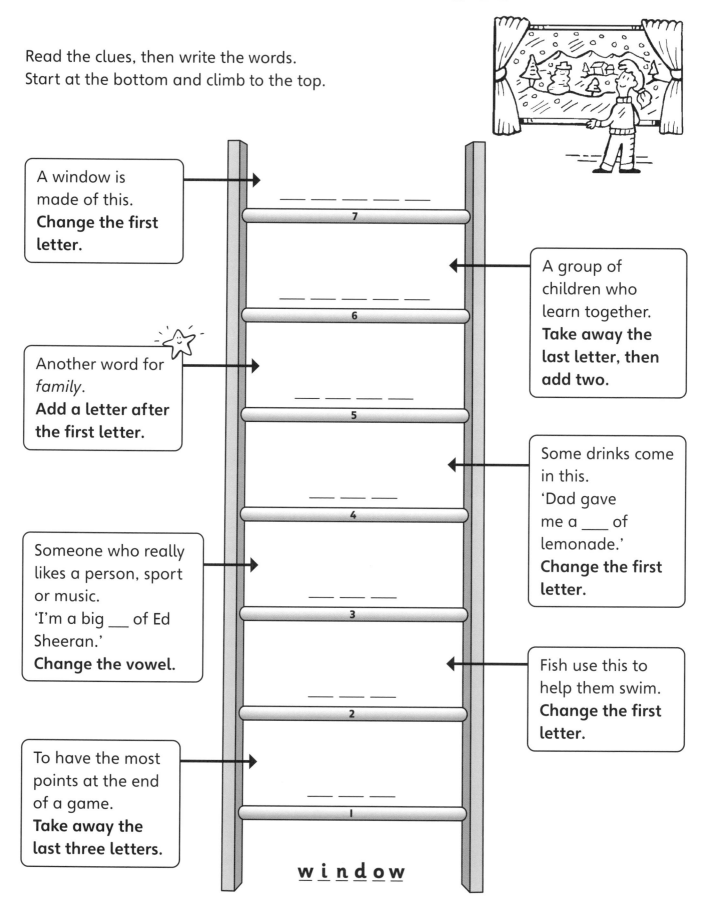

A window is made of this. **Change the first letter.**

→ 7 _ _ _ _ _ _

A group of children who learn together. **Take away the last letter, then add two.** ←

6 _ _ _ _ _ _

Another word for *family*. **Add a letter after the first letter.**

→ 5 _ _ _ _ _

Some drinks come in this. 'Dad gave me a ___ of lemonade.' **Change the first letter.** ←

4 _ _ _ _

Someone who really likes a person, sport or music. 'I'm a big ___ of Ed Sheeran.' **Change the vowel.**

→ 3 _ _ _

Fish use this to help them swim. **Change the first letter.** ←

2 _ _ _ _

To have the most points at the end of a game. **Take away the last three letters.**

→ 1 _ _ _ _

<u>w i n d o w</u>

Name _____

Just for you

Read the clues, then write the words.
Start at the bottom and climb to the top.

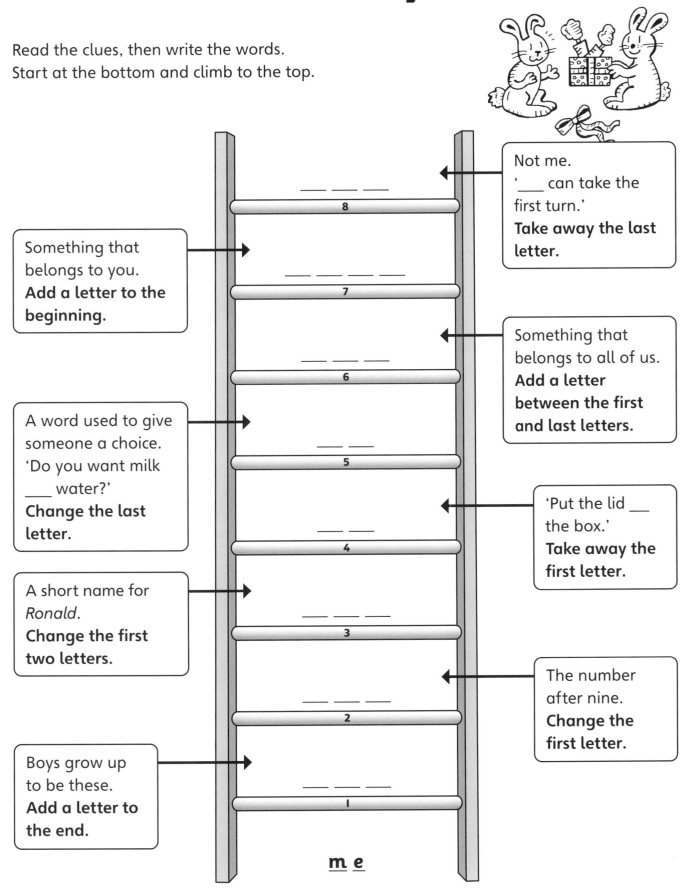

8 _ _ _ _

Not me.
'___ can take the first turn.'
Take away the last letter.

Something that belongs to you.
Add a letter to the beginning.

7 _ _ _ _ _

6 _ _ _ _

Something that belongs to all of us.
Add a letter between the first and last letters.

A word used to give someone a choice.
'Do you want milk ___ water?'
Change the last letter.

5 _ _

4 _ _ _

'Put the lid ___ the box.'
Take away the first letter.

A short name for *Ronald*.
Change the first two letters.

3 _ _ _ _

The number after nine.
Change the first letter.

Boys grow up to be these.
Add a letter to the end.

2 _ _ _

1 _ _ _

<u>m</u> <u>e</u>

Photocopiable

Name _____

A bundle of surprises

Read the clues, then write the words.
Start at the bottom and climb to the top.

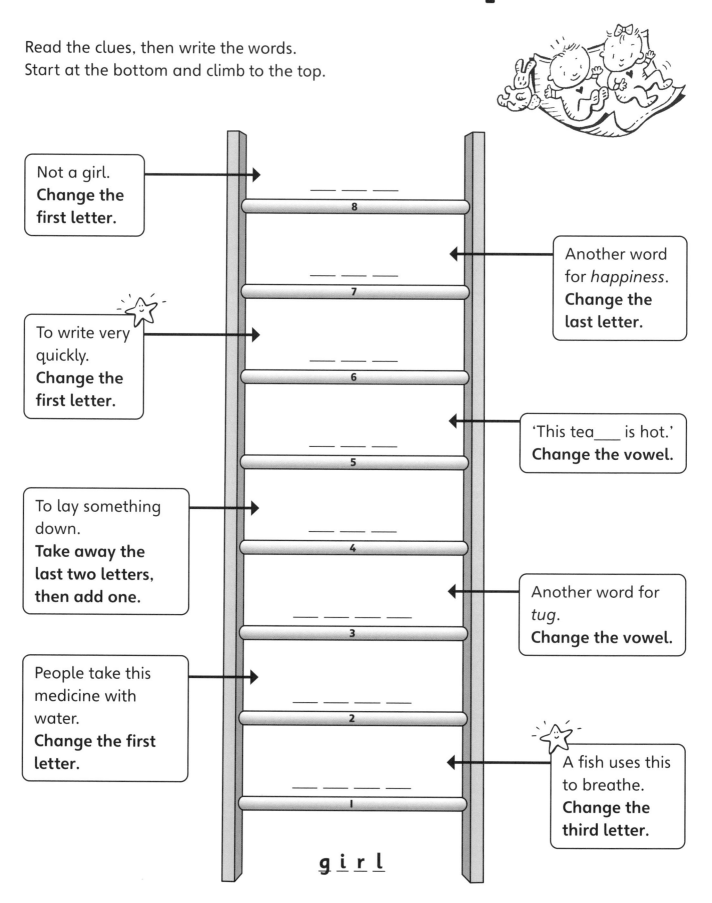

Not a girl. **Change the first letter.**
→ 8 _ _ _ _

← Another word for *happiness*. **Change the last letter.**
7 _ _ _ _

To write very quickly. **Change the first letter.**
→ 6 _ _ _ _

← 'This tea___ is hot.' **Change the vowel.**
5 _ _ _ _

To lay something down. **Take away the last two letters, then add one.**
→ 4 _ _ _ _

← Another word for *tug*. **Change the vowel.**
3 _ _ _ _ _

People take this medicine with water. **Change the first letter.**
→ 2 _ _ _ _

← A fish uses this to breathe. **Change the third letter.**
1 _ _ _ _

g i r l

Photocopiable

Daily Word Ladders for Fluency ■SCHOLASTIC

Name _____

Better and better

Read the clues, then write the words.
Start at the bottom and climb to the top.

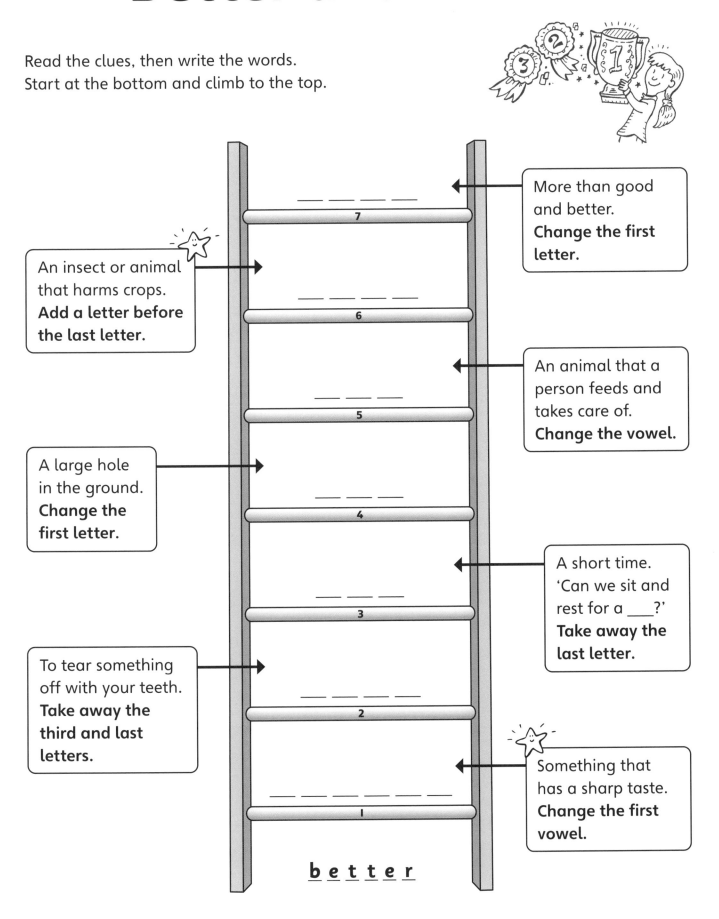

More than good and better. **Change the first letter.**

An insect or animal that harms crops. **Add a letter before the last letter.**

An animal that a person feeds and takes care of. **Change the vowel.**

A large hole in the ground. **Change the first letter.**

A short time. 'Can we sit and rest for a ___?' **Take away the last letter.**

To tear something off with your teeth. **Take away the third and last letters.**

Something that has a sharp taste. **Change the first vowel.**

b e t t e r

Boo!

Read the clues, then write the words.
Start at the bottom and climb to the top.

To do something special for someone. **Change the first letter.**

Another word for *fantastic*. **Rearrange the letters.**

To shred cheese into small pieces. **Take away the first letter, then add two.**

Opposite of *early*. **Change the third letter.**

String that you use to tie up a shoe. **Take away the first two letters, then add one.**

If you copy a picture, you might ___ it. **Change the last letter.**

A train moves on this. **Change the vowel.**

t r i c k

Up, up and away

Read the clues, then write the words.
Start at the bottom and climb to the top.

8 — — — —

Birds flap their wings to do this. **Take away the first two letters, then add two.**

To do your best. 'I always ___ to write neatly.' **Take away the last two letters, then add one.**

7 — — —

6 — — — — —

Apples grow on this. **Add a letter after the first letter.**

A small wooden peg that holds a golf ball. **Change the first vowel.**

5 — — —

4 — — —

You do this to your shoelaces. **Change the first letter.**

'I helped make an apple ___ for Sunday lunch.' **Change the last letter.**

3 — — —

2 — — —

A deep hole in the ground. **Change the first letter.**

A set of things needed to make something. 'I got a science ___ for my birthday.' **Take away the last letter.**

1 — — —

k i t e

Name _____

Coffee break

Read the clues, then write the words.
Start at the bottom and climb to the top.

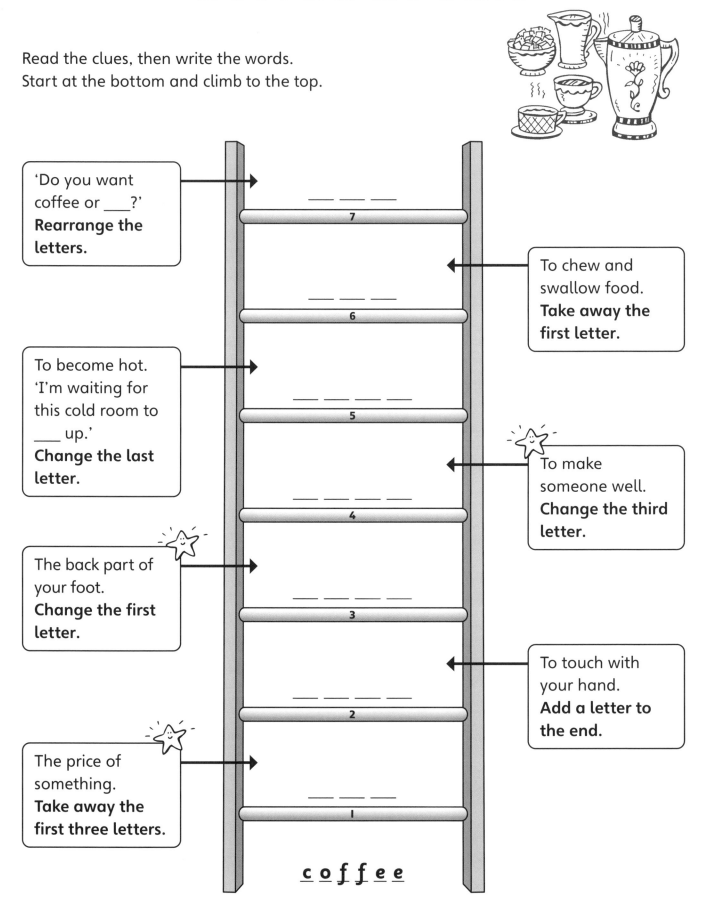

'Do you want coffee or ___?'
Rearrange the letters.

To chew and swallow food.
Take away the first letter.

To become hot. 'I'm waiting for this cold room to ___ up.'
Change the last letter.

To make someone well.
Change the third letter.

The back part of your foot.
Change the first letter.

To touch with your hand.
Add a letter to the end.

The price of something.
Take away the first three letters.

7
6
5
4
3
2
1

c o f f e e

Daily Word Ladders for Fluency **SCHOLASTIC**

Name _____

Greener pastures

Read the clues, then write the words.
Start at the bottom and climb to the top.

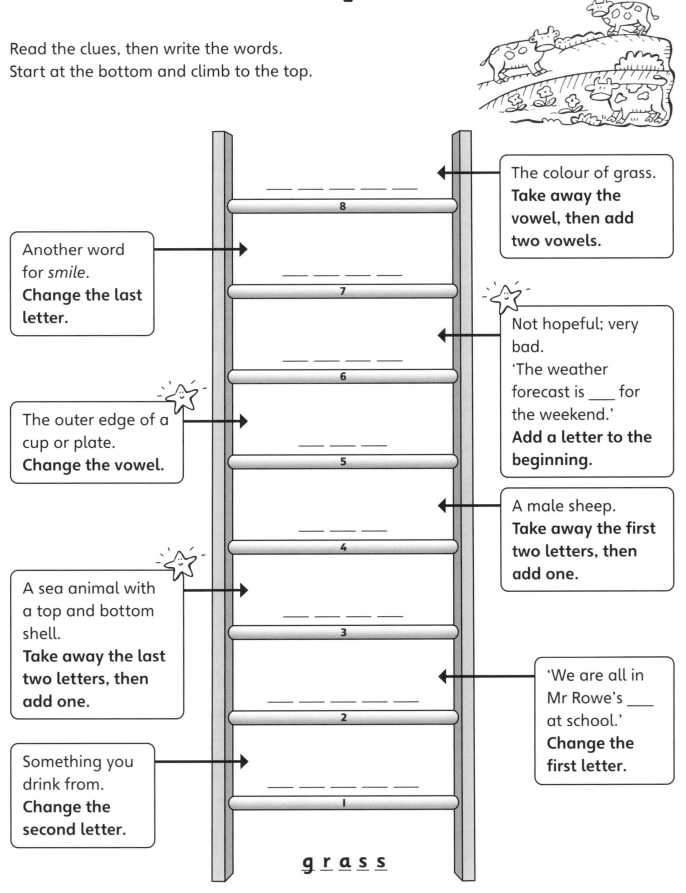

The colour of grass.
Take away the vowel, then add two vowels.

Another word for *smile*.
Change the last letter.

Not hopeful; very bad.
'The weather forecast is ___ for the weekend.'
Add a letter to the beginning.

The outer edge of a cup or plate.
Change the vowel.

A male sheep.
Take away the first two letters, then add one.

A sea animal with a top and bottom shell.
Take away the last two letters, then add one.

'We are all in Mr Rowe's ___ at school.'
Change the first letter.

Something you drink from.
Change the second letter.

8
7
6
5
4
3
2
1

g r a s s

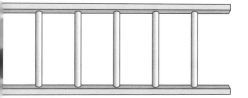

Answers

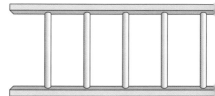

The first word for each page is the bottom of the ladder, the last word is the top of the ladder.

Farm fun (page 8)
cow, cot, pot, pet, pit, pig

Dinner's ready (page 9)
bite, bit, hit, hat, fat, eat

Inside out (page 10)
in, fin, fan, fat, cat, cut, out

Around the clock (page 11)
tick, sick, sack, rack, rock, tock

Animal enemies (page 12)
dog, dot, pot, pop, top, tap, cap, cat

Air travel (page 13)
plane, plan, pan, pen, men, met, jet

Opposites attract (page 14)
fat, fit, hit, his, this, thin

Get well soon (page 15)
ill, pill, hill, sill, silk, sick

Give a dog a bone (page 16)
tail, sail, said, sad, bad, bag, wag

Here to there (page 17)
walk, wall, fall, full, fun, run

Take a seat (page 18)
sit, hit, hat, had, hand, sand, stand

Fur facts (page 19)
hair, hail, fail, fall, ball, bald

Shipshape (page 20)
ship, slip, slap, sap, sat, set, sea

Fancy footwear (page 21)
sock, rock, row, how, show, shoe

Counting up (page 22)
few, dew, den, men, man, many

Personality change (page 23)
good, gold, cold, bold, bald, bad

Frosty fun (page 24)
snow, now, how, hot, hit, white

One more (page 25)
five, hive, hide, hid, hip, sip, six

Under the stars (page 26)
tent, ten, tan, ran, ram, ramp, camp

Baby animals (page 27)
kitten, kite, bite, bit, pit, put, pup

Wildlife (page 28)
bird, bid, bit, fit, fist, fish

Raise your voice (page 29)
talk, tack, tick, pick, pink, sink, sing

Winter wear (page 30)
hand, land, lane, lone, love, glove

Candlelight (page 31)
fire, hire, hare, fare, fame, flame

End of the day (page 32)
work, worm, warm, way, lay, play

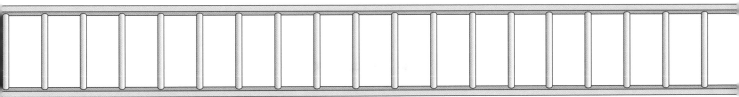

Finish line (page 33)
first, fist, mist, most, lost, last

Stormy days (page 34)
rain, ran, fan, far, for, four, pour

Climbing limbs (page 35)
arm, harm, ham, hum, hug, bug, beg, leg

City living (page 36)
window, win, won, Don, do, door

The whole story (page 37)
start, part, past, pant, ant, and, end

Let's go fishing (page 38)
duck, luck, lick, sick, sink, pink, prank

Blast off! (page 39)
now, not, hot, hat, hate, late, later

Feathered friends (page 40)
duck, luck, lock, lost, lose, loose, goose

In the attic (page 41)
this, his, hit, sit, sat, rat, hat, that

Utensils (page 42)
spoon, spot, pot, port, pork, fork

Happy birthday (page 43)
present, sent, set, let, lit, lift, gift

New and not-so-new (page 44)
new, now, how, hoe, hole, hold, old

In the water (page 45)
float, flat, fat, sat, sack, sick, sink

Quick wit (page 46)
brain, rain, ran, pan, pin, pink, think

All wet (page 47)
cloud, clod, rod, rot, rat, ran, rain

Take a seat (page 48)
table, tale, tall, tail, hail, hair, chair

Woodcutter (page 49)
tree, bee, see, seep, seed, weed, wood

Daily journey (page 50)
school, tool, too, moo, mop, mope, hope, home

Good books (page 51)
book, look, lock, rock, rack, race, rage, page

Furry friends (page 52)
hamster, ham, had, head, hear, tear, tea, pea, pet

Time flies (page 53)
time, tame, tale, talk, tack, tock, lock, clock

Country living (page 54)
farm, harm, hard, card, car, care, bare, barn

Fun for everyone (page 55)
us, bus, but, bat, hat, ham, hem, them

Beautiful day (page 56)
sun, fun, fur, far, fare, fire, fine, shine

Good scents (page 57)
smell, bell, bet, best, pest, post, pose, nose

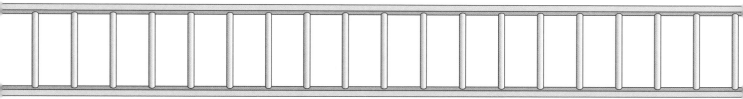

Meadow friends (page 58)
sheep, steep, step, stop, top, pot, got, goat

Gentle breeze (page 59)
wind, find, fine, line, lone, low, bow, blow

Taking a dip (page 60)
swim, slim, slam, clam, cram, cry, fry, fly

Open wide (page 61)
open, pen, pet, pot, post, lost, lose, close

Feelings (page 62)
glad, lad, mad, made, mane, male, mile, smile

Fireworks (page 63)
spark, park, Mark, mare, male, mile, file, fire

On the move (page 64)
bike, like, lake, lame, lamb, lab, cab, car

Car trouble (page 65)
wheel, feel, fell, tell, till, tilt, tile, tyre

Hair care (page 66)
head, read, red, rid, raid, paid, pair, hair

Hungry (page 67)
eat, seat, set, sit, sink, wink, rink, drink

Bookworm (page 68)
read, head, heat, beat, belt, bolt, boot, book

Peaks and valleys (page 69)
high, sigh, sight, sit, hit, hot, how, low

Go, go, go (page 70)
street, tree, see, set, net, not, nod, rod, road

Wild noises (page 71)
bear, ear, are, rare, raw, row, grow, growl

Life saver (page 72)
help, yelp, yell, smell, small, all, ail, aid

Bread and butter (page 73)
bread, read, had, bad, bat, boat, boast, toast

In the sky (page 74)
yellow, yell, bell, bull, but, cut, cue, blue

Sailing (page 75)
sea, seat, beat, bat, mat, mate, make, lake

School days (page 76)
read, real, meal, meat, wheat, what, white, write

Toe-tapping tunes (page 77)
toe, woe, won, win, wing, sing, singer, finger

Wonderful words (page 78)
letter, let, lot, pot, cot, cod, cord, word

On your feet (page 79)
shoe, hoe, hot, hat, rat, rate, race, lace

Time's up (page 80)
early, ear, hear, hare, dare, date, late

Directions (page 81)
north, port, pout, pour, our, out, south

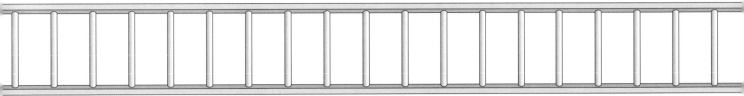

In the tree (page 82)
climb, limb, lime, mile, me, she, see, tree

Brrrrr! (page 83)
cool, spool, spoon, soon, son, sod, sold, cold

A clear view (page 84)
window, win, fin, fan, can, clan, class, glass

Just for you (page 85)
me, men, ten, Ron, on, or, our, your, you

A bundle of surprises (page 86)
girl, gill, pill, pull, put, pot, jot, joy, boy

Better and better (page 87)
better, bitter, bite, bit, pit, pet, pest, best

Boo! (page 88)
trick, track, trace, lace, late, grate, great, treat

Up, up and away (page 89)
kite, kit, pit, pie, tie, tee, tree, try, fly

Coffee break (page 90)
coffee, fee, feel, heel, heal, heat, eat, tea

Greener pastures (page 91)
grass, glass, class, clam, ram, rim, grim, grin, green